Joe Orton

CRIMES OF PASSION:

THE RUFFIAN ON THE STAIR
THE ERPINGHAM CAMP

EYRE METHUEN · LONDON

First published by Methuen and Co Ltd 1967
Reprinted 1972 and 1973
© 1967 by the Estate of Joe Orton, deceased

SBN 413 45190 9

Printed Offset Litho in Great Britain by
COX & WYMAN LTD.
LONDON, FAKENHAM AND READING

ACKNOWLEDGEMENT

The lyric of the song 'My Irish Song of Songs'
is reproduced on page 62 by permission of
B. Feldman & Co. Ltd.

© 1917 M. Whitmark & Sons, New York

To
PETER WILLES

CONTENTS

The Ruffian on the Stair

'Madam Life's a piece in bloom,
Death goes dogging everywhere:
She's the tenant of the room,
He's the ruffian on the stair.'

W. E. HENLEY

The Ruffian on the Stair was given its first stage perform-
ance in a production without decor by the English Stage
Society on 21st August 1966 with the following cast:

MIKE	Bernard Gallagher
JOYCE	Sheila Ballantine
WILSON	Kenneth Cranham

Directed by Peter Gill

The Ruffian on the Stair was later produced at the Royal Court
Theatre on 6th June 1967 in a double-bill entitled *Crimes of
Passion* with the following cast:

MIKE	Bernard Gallagher
JOYCE	Avril Elgar
WILSON	Michael Standing

Directed by Peter Gill
Designed by Deirdre Clancy

SCENE ONE

A kitchen/living-room with a bedroom alcove. MIKE *is shaving by the sink.* JOYCE *enters from the bedroom carrying a tray with cups, saucers, egg cup, etc. She puts the tray on to the table.*

JOYCE. Have you got an appointment today?

MIKE. Yes. I'm to be at King's Cross station at eleven. I'm meeting a man in the toilet.

He puts away his shaving materials.

JOYCE. You always go to such interesting places. Are you taking the van?

MIKE *puts on a made-up bow tie.*

MIKE. No. It's still under repair.

JOYCE *takes the tray to the sink and puts the dishes into a bowl. She pours water on them.*

JOYCE (*putting on a pair of rubber gloves*). Where did you go yesterday?

MIKE. I went to Mickey Pierce's. I'd a message to deliver. I had a chat with a man who travels in electrically operated massage machines. He bought me a ham roll. It turns out he's on the run. He didn't say as much in so many words. (*He winks.*) But I gathered.

JOYCE. A wanted man?

MIKE. I don't suppose his firm would pay the insurance if they realised his position.

JOYCE. No.

She begins to wash the dishes. MIKE *puts on his coat.*

JOYCE. You lead a more interesting life than I do.

MIKE. Hard, though.

JOYCE. Still, you've kept your looks.

MIKE. Yes. I'm a powerfully attractive figure. I can still cause a flutter in feminine hearts.

He puts a flower into his buttonhole, and brushes his coat down.

JOYCE. Have you seen the date?

MIKE. No.

JOYCE. It's our anniversary.

MIKE. As long as that, is it? How time flies.

JOYCE. Two years ago you came to my flat and persuaded me to give up the life I'd been leading.

MIKE. You're better off.

JOYCE. Nobody ever calls me Maddy now.

MIKE (*pause*). What?

JOYCE. Nobody calls me Madelein. I used that name for five years. Before that I was Sarah up North somewhere.

MIKE (*pause, he frowns*). Have you ever, since I met you, allowed another man to be intimate with you?

JOYCE. No!

MIKE. Good. I'd kill any man who messed with you. Oh, yes. I'd murder him.

Silence.

JOYCE (*taking off her rubber gloves*). The papers were on form this morning.

MIKE. Were they? I'm glad people are still reading them.

JOYCE. I see where a man has appeared in court charged with locking his wife in a wardrobe. She tells of her night of terror. (*Pause.*) What a way to celebrate your wedding anniversary.

MIKE *picks up his raincoat and folds it across his arm.*

MIKE. I'd do the same. I'd lock you up if you gave me cause for displeasure.

JOYCE. And, in the local paper, I saw there'd been an accident involving a tattooed man. He had a heart, a clenched fist and a rose all on one arm. And the name 'Ronny' was on his body in two different places.

MIKE. Was that his name?

JOYCE. No. His name was Frank. A van ran him down.

Silence.

MIKE. I'm going now.

JOYCE. Are your boots clean?

MIKE. Yes.

JOYCE. Keep them clean. You may meet important people. You never know.

MIKE. Cheerio.

JOYCE. Give me a kiss. (*He kisses her cheek.*) Do I have to remind you now? Two years ago you did it without thinking.

MIKE. I was young then. See you tonight.

He exits. JOYCE *goes into the bedroom, straightens the bed. She pushes* MIKE'S *pyjamas under the pillow. The doorbell rings. She answers it.* WILSON *is standing outside.*

WILSON (*smiling*). I've come about the room.

JOYCE. I'm afraid there's been a mistake. I've nothing to do with allotting rooms. Make your enquiries elsewhere.

WILSON. I'm not coloured. I was brought up in the Home Counties.

JOYCE. That doesn't ring a bell with me, I'm afraid.

WILSON. Is that the room?

JOYCE. That's my room.

WILSON. I couldn't share. What rent are you asking?

JOYCE. I'm not asking any.

WILSON. I don't want charity. I'd pay for my room.

JOYCE. You must've come to the wrong door. I'm sorry you've been troubled.

She tries to close the door, but WILSON *blocks it with his foot.*

WILSON. Can I come in? I've walked all the way here. (*Pause. He smiles.*)

JOYCE. Just for a minute.

She lets him in and closes the door. He sits down.

I'm so busy. I'm run off my feet today.

WILSON. How about a cup of tea? You usually make one about now.

JOYCE *nods. She goes to the sink but is pulled up sharp.*

JOYCE. How do you know?

WILSON. Oh, I pick up all sorts of useful information in my job.

JOYCE. What's that?

She pours water from the kettle into the teapot.

WILSON. I'm a Gents hairdresser. Qualified. My dad has a business. Just a couple of chairs. I've clipped some notable heads in my time. Mostly professional men. Though we had an amateur street musician in a few weeks ago. We gave him satisfaction, I believe.

JOYCE *puts out two cups and pours his tea.*

WILSON. My brother was in the business too. Until he was involved in an accident.

He puts sugar into his tea and milk.

JOYCE. What happened?

WILSON. A van knocked him down.

JOYCE *pours her own tea.*

JOYCE. Was he tattooed?

WILSON. You've heard of him?

JOYCE. I've heard of his tattoos.

WILSON. They were unique. He had them done by a well-known artist. (*He takes a biscuit from the barrel.*) His funeral was attended by some interesting people. He was a sports-man before his decease. He wore white shorts better than any man I've ever come in contact with. As a matter of fact, strictly off the record, I'm wearing a pair of his white shorts at this moment. They're inconvenient ... because ... (*He blurts it out.*) – there's no fly. (*Pause.*) He wore them two days before he was killed.

JOYCE *looks away in a brief spasm of embarrassment which quickly passes.*

I wasn't mentioned in the press. They didn't realise the

important part I played in Frank's life. So I didn't get the coverage. I thought of revealing myself. But what's the good? (*Pause.*) My brother's fiancée had her photo taken. Bawling her head off. She insisted we bury the engagement ring with him. It was just an idle, theatrical gesture. It's too much trouble now to put a bunch of flowers on the grave.

JOYCE. Perhaps the accident unhinged her mind.

WILSON. It wasn't an accident. (*He drinks his tea.*) He was murdered.

JOYCE. You don't know that.

WILSON. Don't contradict me!

JOYCE *stares in surprise.*

JOYCE (*angry*). This is a private house. What do you mean by raising your voice? I'm not having perfect strangers talking to me like that.

WILSON *drinks his tea and eats a biscuit.*

Drink that tea and clear off. I don't want to see you here again. My husband will be back soon.

WILSON. He's not your husband.

JOYCE (*furious*). How dare you. You've gone too far. Leave my room at once.

WILSON. You're not married. You want to watch yourself.

JOYCE. I've a good mind to call a policeman.

WILSON. You aren't on the phone.

JOYCE. I can knock on the floor.

WILSON. There's nobody downstairs.

JOYCE. I'll report you.

WILSON *stands to his feet.*

WILSON. Come here.

JOYCE (*alarmed*). Keep away!

WILSON *looks at her, cup in hand. He takes a sip of tea.*

WILSON. Do you know I could murder you. Easy as that. (*He snaps his fingers.*) That's how these assaults on lonely women are all committed. I could make a very nasty attack on you at this moment. If I was so inclined.

JOYCE (*with a note of hysteria*). Don't come any nearer.

WILSON. Is your husband passionate with you?

JOYCE *draws in a sharp breath.*

JOYCE. I'm reporting you. Using filthy language.

WILSON. If I were to assault you would he avenge it?

JOYCE. Yes.

WILSON. Where does he keep his gun?

JOYCE. He hasn't got a gun.

WILSON. I have it on good authority that he keeps it loaded.

He takes a step towards her. She backs away.

Where is it?

JOYCE. In the drawer. Over there.

WILSON *goes to the drawer. He puts down his cup, opens the drawer and takes out a revolver. He checks that it is loaded, puts it back into the drawer and closes the drawer. Then he walks back to the table with the cup in his hand and drinks the last of his tea, placing the cup back on to the saucer.*

WILSON (*smiling*). Thanks for the tea.

JOYCE *stares, puzzled.*

JOYCE. Are you going?

WILSON. The room's not available, is it? I expect you think I'm Jewish or something. (*Pause.*) Have you got a couple of bob to spare? I can't walk all the way back.

JOYCE *opens her handbag.*

JOYCE (*giving him money*). Here's half-a-crown. Don't let me see you round here again.

WILSON *goes off.* JOYCE *takes a bottle of pills from her handbag and swallows several.*

SCENE TWO

Later.

The remains of an evening meal are on the table. MIKE *is smoking a small cigar.* JOYCE *is reading a book. She has a pair of glasses on.*

MIKE. I went to the King's Cross toilet like I told you. I met my contact. He was a man with bad feet. He looked as though life had treated him rough. He hadn't much to live for. I gave him the message from the – er – (*Pause.*) The message was delivered. I went outside on to the platform. It was cold. I saw an old girl hardly able to breathe. Had something wrong with her. Hardly able to breathe. Her face was blue. (*Pause.*) Are you listening, Joycie?

JOYCE (*taking off her glasses, and putting her book down*). Yes. (*Pause.*) I've had a busy day.

MIKE. Are you tired?

JOYCE. A bit.

MIKE. Have a busy day, did you?

JOYCE (*sharply*). Yes. Why don't you listen? You never listen to anyone but yourself.

MIKE. I do.

JOYCE. You never listen to me.

MIKE. You never say anything interesting.

JOYCE. I might as well be dead. (*Pause.*) What if you came home and I was dead?

MIKE. Are you queer?

JOYCE. No.

MIKE (*pause*). Is your insides playing you up?

JOYCE. I'm all right.

MIKE. Is your liver upset then?

JOYCE. No.

MIKE. It's that fried food you eat. You wolf it down. Put something in the pan and have a fry. That's your motto.

JOYCE. You seem to thrive on it.

MIKE. I'm a man. A man has different glands. You can't go on what I eat.

JOYCE. Oh, well, if you must know, I think it's my nerves.

MIKE. You can't die of nerves.

JOYCE. Can't you?

MIKE. I'm going to the free library tomorrow. I'll look it up.

JOYCE (*pause*). What if I were done in?

MIKE. Who'd do you in?

JOYCE. Somebody might. You read of attacks every day on lonely defenceless women.

MIKE. You could call for help.

JOYCE. Who to?

MIKE. Mary.

JOYCE. She's not in. She's working again. I'm alone in the house.

MIKE. You could break a window. That would attract attention.

JOYCE (*pause*). Don't go out tomorrow.

MIKE. I can't mope around here. I'm active. It gets on my tits.

> JOYCE *closes her book, marking the place.* MIKE *begins to clear the supper things away and puts them into the sink.*

Mary used to be on her own. She was all right.

JOYCE. Mary can cope.

> MIKE *turns from the sink.*

MIKE. And why's that? Because she's a Catholic. She carries her Faith into her private life. That's what we're taught to do. We don't always succeed. But we try.

> *He takes off his coat.*

Why don't you have a chat with Mary? She'd put you right. Give you the address of a priest with an enquiring mind. He'd stop your maundering.

> *He takes off his shoes.*

You've a vivid imagination. A fertile mind. An asset in some people. But in your case it's not. (*Pause.*) It's in the mind. That's what the Father would say. You'd be better if you'd accept the Communion. That's what you need. I've said so for years.

JOYCE. I'd still be alone.

MIKE. You'd have the Sacrament inside you. That would be something. (*Pause.*) Anyway who'd assault you? Who? He'd

have to be out of his mind. Look at your face. When did
it last see water?

JOYCE. I've been crying.

MIKE. Crying? Are you pregnant?

JOYCE. No. I'm worried.

MIKE. No one would be interested in assaulting you. It's pride
to think they would. The idea is farcical. Please don't
burden me with it.

*He takes off his bow tie, goes into the bedroom, turns back
the sheets and picks up his pyjamas.*

JOYCE *comes to the bedroom entrance.*

JOYCE. Mike . . . (*Pause.*) A kid came here today.

MIKE *takes off his waistcoat.*

MIKE. One of the Teds?

JOYCE. No. He tried to molest me.

MIKE. These kids see you coming. Why didn't you call for
Mary?

JOYCE. She's not in! She's not in! Do I talk for the sake of it?
(*Pause.*) Mike . . . If he pays another visit – what shall I
do? Give me a word of advice?

MIKE *unbuttons his shirt.*

MIKE. Bring me my overcoat, will you? It's raw tonight.
We'll need extra on the bed.

SCENE THREE

Morning.

JOYCE *pauses in cleaning the room.*

JOYCE. I can't go to the park. I can't sit on cold stone. I might
get piles from the lowered temperature. I wouldn't want
them on top of everything else.

She puts down the duster, apathetically.

I'd try, maybe, a prayer. But the Virgin would turn a deaf
ear to a Protestant. (*Pause.*) I can't be as alone as all that.
Nobody ought to be. It's heartbreaking.

She listens. There is silence.

The number of humiliating admissions I've made. You'd think it would draw me closer to somebody. But it doesn't.

Three short rings are given on the doorbell.

Who's there?

No answer.

What do you want? (*Making up her mind.*) I'll answer the door to no one. They can hammer it down. (*Pause.*) Is it the milk? (*Calling.*) Are you deaf? No, it wouldn't be him. He only rings for his money.

She stands behind the door.

(*Loudly.*) Are you the insurance? (*Pause.*) But he comes on Friday. This is a Wednesday.

She backs away from the door, anxious.

Nobody comes of a Wednesday. (*She bends down and peeps through the letter-box.*) If it's my money you're after, there's not a thing in my purse.

She bites her lip, standing in thought.

(*Loudly.*) Are you from the Assistance? They come any time. I've had them on Monday. They come whenever they choose. It's their right. (*With a smile and growing confidence.*) You're the Assistance, aren't you? (*Her voice rises.*) Are you or aren't you?

> *Glass is heard breaking from the bedroom. She runs to the entrance of the bedroom and leaps back, startled; a piece of brick has been thrown through the window.* JOYCE *stares, her mouth trembling. Another piece of brick hurtles through the window, smashing another pane.*

(*Screaming.*) It's him! He's breaking in. God Almighty, what shall I do? He'll murder me!

She stamps on the floor.

Mary! Mary!

> *She runs to the door, opens it and runs out into the passage. Her frantic tones can be heard crying:*

Mrs O'Connor! Mrs O'Connor!

She runs back into the room; slams the door shut. The lock drops with a crash on to the floor. She picks it up and stares at it and then shrieks with fright.

It's come off! It's broke!

She tries to fit the lock back on to the door.

I've told him so often. I've – told him to – mend it!

She gives up, breathless. Then she tries to pull the settee out into the room, but gives up and picks up a chair which she pushes against the door and sits on.

He'll easily fling this aside. Oh, Michael, I'm to be murdered because you're too bone idle to fix a lock.

There is a prolonged ringing on the doorbell.

Let me alone! I'm going to report you. I've seen them at the station. They've set a trap. I'm safe in here. We have an extremely strong and reliable Chubb lock on the door. So you're trapped. Ha, ha! The detectives are watching the house.

The front door is kicked. The chair pushes away and JOYCE *is flung aside. She backs into the bedroom.*

If it's the gun you want, I don't know where he's put it. He's taken it. (*Pause.*) I may be able to find it. Is that what you want?

Outside the door a burst of music is heard from a transistor radio. There is knocking. The bell rings. A sudden silence. Laughter. Silence. A splintering of wood.

(JOYCE *calls shrilly.*) I've told my hubby. He's seeing someone. You'll laugh on the other side of your face.

Suddenly, giving up all pretence, she bursts into tears.

Go away. There's a good boy. I don't know what you want. I've no money. Please go away. Please, please, please ... (*She sobs.*)

SCENE FOUR

Later.
MIKE *sits at the table reading a newspaper.* JOYCE *enters in outdoor clothes.*

MIKE. Where've you been? (*He folds up the paper.*)
　　JOYCE *takes off her hat and coat and puts them into the wardrobe.*
JOYCE. Out.
MIKE. Out? What about my tea? It wasn't ready.
JOYCE. I've been walking round. I didn't come back till I saw the light in the window.
MIKE. Where did you go?
JOYCE. Into Woolworths.
MIKE. What for?
JOYCE. The people. The lights. The crowds. (*Pause.*) That kid came again. He broke two windows today in the bedroom.
MIKE. I thought it was them next door.
JOYCE. Have you seen the banisters? Smashed to bits. Wantonness. I couldn't stop him. (*Lowering her voice.*) He pissed on the floor in the passage. I had to clean it up. Been ringing the doorbell half the day. Running up and down the stairs. I'm nearly out of my mind. It didn't stop till four. (*Pause.*) I can hardly think with worry.
MIKE. Did you witness him?
JOYCE. I was in here.
MIKE. Did you see him?
JOYCE (*furiously*). I won't stand it. I want something done. Look at that lock. Why don't you mend it?
MIKE. I'll try and borrow a set of screws.
JOYCE. You can decide what you're doing. I can't keep pace with the excitement. I'll be in a home.
MIKE. Did he try to get into the room?

JOYCE. No.

MIKE. Could he have got in if he'd wanted?

JOYCE (*pause*). Yes.

MIKE. Did he speak?

JOYCE. No.

MIKE. Then how d'you know it was him from yesterday? If you didn't see him and he didn't speak? How d'you know?
Silence.

JOYCE. It must be the same man.

MIKE. Why didn't you go outside and see?

JOYCE. He'd've killed me.

MIKE. How do you know that? You've no evidence to support your theory.

JOYCE. But . . . (*Wide-eyed.*) . . . I'd be dead if I'd got evidence.

MIKE. I'd prosecute him on your behalf, Joycie.
JOYCE *blows her nose; she doesn't speak.*

JOYCE (*at last, wearily*). Will you mend the lock for me? I'll feel safer then.

MIKE. I'll see to it when I get back.
He goes into the bedroom and picks up his coat from the end of the bed.

JOYCE. Back? Back from where?

MIKE (*entering, putting on his coat*). I'm seeing a man who could put me in touch with something.
He goes to the sink and puts the flower into his buttonhole.

JOYCE. I'll go down to Mary. (*Pause.*) Would you like a bikky before you go?

MIKE. No, I'll have something on the way.

JOYCE. Is it important tonight?

MIKE. I may be employed to do another job in the van. We're fixing the details.
The doorbell is rung violently. MIKE *puts the silver paper from the flower into the waste bin.*

MIKE. Is that the bell?

JOYCE. Yes.

MIKE (*going into the bedroom*). Answer it then. I'm here with you.

> *The bell is rung again.* MIKE *takes the packet of cigarettes from the drawer and fills his cigarette case.* JOYCE *opens the door.* WILSON *is outside.*

WILSON (*smiling*). Are you the lady I saw yesterday?

JOYCE. It's you!

WILSON. You are the lady?

JOYCE. What do you mean by pestering me?

WILSON. There's no need to raise your voice.

JOYCE. My husband is in. Coming here, trying your tricks. Making a nuisance. I've only to call and he'll soon put a stop to you. Do you understand?

WILSON. I'm afraid I don't.

JOYCE. Coming here playing me up. What do you mean by it? It's disgusting. Anyone would think you were a kid. Behaving like that. You know what I mean, don't you? You know. Like an animal. (*Pause.*) Are you paying for those windows?

WILSON. I don't know what you're talking about.

JOYCE. You're a liar! A bloody little liar!

WILSON. Don't speak to me like that, lady. I'm not used to it.

JOYCE. I've had enough. I'm putting a stop to this. (*Calls.*) Michael!

> MIKE *enters from the bedroom. He slips his cigarette case into his pocket.*

JOYCE. Come here. (*To* WILSON.) Stay where you are! Stay here!

> *She attempts to grab his arm. He tries to shake her off. She hangs on. He shrugs her away, violently. She comes back. They struggle.* MIKE *goes to the mirror and runs a comb through his hair.*

JOYCE (*shouting excited*). Mike! Michael! (*To* WILSON.) I'll have my husband to you. (*Turning, excited.*) Where are you, Michael! For God's sake!

MIKE *puts the comb away and strolls to the door.*

MIKE (*coolly*). What's the matter?

JOYCE. This is him. The one that's been coming here.

MIKE (*to* WILSON). What's this, I hear? Have you been annoying my wife?

JOYCE. Yes. He has.

MIKE (*to* JOYCE). Let's hear his version of it. (*To* WILSON.) Tell me the truth.

WILSON. I wanted a room.

MIKE. We haven't got a room.

WILSON. You're Irish! My mother was Irish. My father was Mediterranean. I have difficulty with rooms for that reason. (*Smiles.*) I've walked all the way from the bus station by Victoria. Do you know that district at all?

MIKE. I know King's Cross intimately.

WILSON. Victoria is a different place entirely. In the summer it has a character of its own. Are you a Londoner?

MIKE. No. I was born in the shadow of the hills of Donegal. We had a peat farm. It was the aftermath of the troubles drove us away. Otherwise there'd be people called Mike in Donegal to this day.

WILSON. I love Ireland. I'd go there tomorrow if it wasn't for my dad. He's a hard man to please. My feet are killing me. Could I have a drink of water?

MIKE. Certainly. Come on in.

JOYCE. You're not letting him in?

MIKE. Be quiet. You're making yourself look ridiculous. (*To* WILSON.) This way. And take no notice of her. She can't help herself.

He leads the way into the room.

Get the lad a glass of water, Joycie.

JOYCE *goes to the sink and fills a glass with water.*

(*To* WILSON.) What part of Ireland is your mother from?

WILSON. Sligo.

MIKE. I once knew a lad from Sligo. Name of Murphy. I wonder if maybe your Ma would've come across him?

WILSON. I'll make enquiries.

MIKE. I'd be obliged if you would. He had dark curly hair and talked with a pronounced brogue. Not an easy man to miss in a crowd.

>   JOYCE *hands* WILSON *the glass of water.*

JOYCE (*to* MIKE). What did you let him in for?

MIKE. He isn't a leper.

JOYCE. Ask him.

MIKE. What?

JOYCE. Ask him about his conduct. He won't be able to face it out.

MIKE (*to* WILSON). About these things she tells me. Did you cheek her yesterday?

WILSON. It depends on which way you look at it. I thought my behaviour was exemplary.

MIKE. Did you molest her?

WILSON (*to* JOYCE). What've you been telling him? I never tried to interfere with you, did I?

JOYCE (*angry*). Stop using that kind of talk. (*To* MIKE.) You can see what I had to put up with.

MIKE. That's medical talk, Joycie. You should learn to control your temper. (*To* WILSON.) Why did you bring a suitcase with you?

WILSON. I wanted a room. (*Nods to* JOYCE.) I thought she might change her mind.

JOYCE. Who's she? The cat's mother.

MIKE (*to* WILSON). Bring it in. You don't want to leave it lying out there.

>   WILSON *exits.*

JOYCE. What are you playing at? After what he's done to me?

MIKE. Quiet!

JOYCE. What's his background? He could be anything.

MIKE. Give the lad a chance.

JOYCE. Chance? After what I've been through?

MIKE. Shut up!

JOYCE (*bewildered*). Shut up?

MIKE. You're heading for a belt around the ear. Go to Mary. Are you going?

> WILSON *enters with a suitcase.*

MIKE. Put it over there, lad. How about a cup of tea, Joycie?

> JOYCE *goes into the bedroom.*

MIKE. She's taken offence. (*Calls.*) Did you hear me? Why don't you show a few manners? (*To* WILSON.) What's your profession?

WILSON. I'm a Gents Hairdresser.

MIKE. You wouldn't have to be dabbling with birth-control devices? That's no way for a Catholic to carry on.

WILSON. I don't handle that part of the trade. My old man does it. He has the free-thinking frame of mind. I can't approve, of course. It's the Latin temperament which has been the curse of our religion all along.

MIKE. The Pope is Italian.

WILSON. You have something there. I'd like to see a Liffey man on the throne of St Peter myself. I'd be proud to hear the Lateran ring with the full-throated blasphemies of our native land.

MIKE. What are you thinking of? The Vicar of Christ doesn't blaspheme.

WILSON. He would if he was Irish and drank Guinness.

MIKE. You're a lad after my own heart. You'll not know me by name, I suppose?

WILSON. I didn't quite catch it.

MIKE. Michael O'Rourke. I was known as Mike or Mickey O'Rourke in the days when you were a nipper. I used to be respected in the boxing profession. I was thought to be heading for the top at one time. Then I had my trouble. (*He turns to the bedroom and calls.*) Isn't that right? Wasn't I handy with my fists then? In the days after the second German war? (*Turns back to* WILSON.) Ignorant cow. (*Into bedroom.*) Are you going to behave decent?

JOYCE *is sitting on the bed. She gives a toss of her head.*

WILSON. I'll go.

MIKE. Don't let her drive you away. You stay.

JOYCE *picks up a cardigan. She enters from the bedroom.*

JOYCE (*in a tight, angry voice*). I'm going downstairs!

She goes off into the hall, slamming the door behind her.

MIKE. Take no notice. She'll come round. She's nervous, you know. It's the life she led before I took up with her. I have to watch her. She'd get me into all sorts of trouble. She has no religious feelings. That's the worst of it. She never had the benefit of the upbringing.

WILSON. My mum was brought up by nuns.

MIKE. Is she still alive?

WILSON. She's in hospital with an infectious disease of the hip-joint. The nuns think the world of her.

MIKE. Is she in pain?

WILSON. She screams out. It's terrible to hear her.

MIKE. I wish I could do something. Would it be any use to burn a candle? I don't think I've the cash on me.

WILSON. Wouldn't the priest lend you the cash?

MIKE. I'd not like to ask. I'd pop across and burn a candle myself. But he might ask questions. It's his business, of course. He's a right to ask. But why should I subject myself to scrutiny? (*Pause.*) Is your mother expected to recover?

WILSON. It's touch and go.

MIKE. She's maybe doomed. She's likely to be a candle herself already. She's probably being stripped by the angels as we speak. I suppose we are roasted nude? I've never seen fit to ask. It's not a question you can put to the Father. Though he is a Jesuit. And that makes a difference. (*Pause.*) Is your da in good health?

WILSON. He's fine. (*Pause.*) I'm not keeping you, am I? ....

MIKE. No. (*Pause, looks at his watch.*) As a matter of fact you've kept me. I've missed my appointment. I shall have to drop them a line and apologise for my absence.

He takes off his coat, puts the flower from his buttonhole into a glass, and puts water into the glass.

(*Putting the glass on to the draining board*). If you're desperate for a room we could put you up. On the bed-settee. It's quite comfortable.

WILSON. Is it new?

MIKE. No.

WILSON. You surprise me.

MIKE. I bought it a long time ago. I couldn't afford such luxury today. Financially I'm in a bad way.

WILSON. Well, my money will help you out.

MIKE. It's the Assistance Board. I'm not a believer in charity. Unless I need it. With the cost of living being so high I'm greatly in need of a weekly donation from the Government. They say my circumstances have altered. I haven't any circumstances to alter. They should know that. I've filled in a form to the effect that I'm a derelict.

WILSON. Yes. My brother and me had the same trouble.

MIKE. They haven't the insight into the human heart that we have in Ireland.

WILSON. We lived in Shepherd's Bush. We had a little room. And our life was made quite comfortable by the N.A.B. for almost a year. We had a lot of friends. All creeds and colours. But no circumstances at all. We were happy, though. We were young. I was seventeen. He was twenty-three. You can't do better for yourself than that, can you? (*He shrugs.*) We were bosom friends. I've never told anyone that before. I hope I haven't shocked you.

MIKE. As close as that?

WILSON. We had separate beds – he was a stickler for convention, but that's as far as it went. We spent every night in each other's company. It was the reason we never got any work done.

MIKE: There's no word in the Irish language for what you were doing.

WILSON. In Lapland they have no word for snow.

MIKE. I'd rather not hear. I'm not a priest, you know.

WILSON. I wasn't with him when he died. I'm going round the twist with heartbreak.

MIKE. He's dead?

WILSON. Yes. I thought of topping myself. As a gesture. I would've done but for my strict upbringing. Suicide is difficult when you've got a pious mum.

MIKE. Kill yourself?

WILSON. I don't want to live, see. That's a crude way of putting it. I've lived among rough people.

MIKE. You won't do it, though?

WILSON. No. I've made a will, of course. In case anything should happen in the future.

MIKE. What might happen?

WILSON. I might get killed.

MIKE. How?

WILSON. I don't know. (*Pause.*) In my will I state that I want to be buried with Frank. It's my last request. They'll be bound to honour it. His fiancée won't mind. She's off already with another man. He's not cold and already it's too much trouble for her to put a bunch of flowers on his grave. She's a typical woman. You've met with it yourself?

MIKE. I have. Some of them are unholy bitches.

WILSON. He wouldn't have benefited from her. I was more intimate with him than she was. I used to base my life round him. You don't often get that, do you?

MIKE (*uneasily*). No.

WILSON. I heard he was a friend of yours. You were pointed out as a man that knew him.

He takes a snapshot from his pocket and hands it to MIKE.

Recognise him?

MIKE *looks at the snapshot.*

MIKE (*pause*). He was nice looking.

WILSON. He had personality. That indefinable something. That was taken two days before he was killed. (*Pause.*) What's the matter? The light hurting your eyes.

MIKE *hands the snapshot back.*

MIKE. Take it away. It upsets me. The thought of him being dead. He was so young.

WILSON. Do you recognise him?

MIKE. I may have seen him once or twice. I may have spoken to him.

WILSON. A van knocked him down.

MIKE (*pause*). Did he say anything? Was there a death-bed scene?

WILSON. He was killed instantaneous. (*Pause.*) You recently had a smash-up in your van, didn't you? I checked with the garage. You've had five major repair jobs in under two years. Why don't you learn to drive properly? You're a disgrace to your profession.

MIKE. I feel bad. I'll have to ask you to go now. It's embarrassing to be ill in a stranger's presence.

WILSON *smiles.*

WILSON. I was going to live here, I thought.

MIKE. I've just realised. We can't put you up.

WILSON. Why not?

MIKE. Her aunt may drop in. I'm sorry I raised your hopes.

WILSON. Does she usually come this late?

MIKE. She does.

WILSON. She must be an ignorant kind of woman, turning up in the middle of the night. No consideration for others. What's her name?

MIKE. Snell.

WILSON. What's her first name?

MIKE. Bridie Francine. She uses the second. Everyone knows Francine Snell.

WILSON. I haven't had the pleasure. What does she look like?

MIKE. She has a growth on the side of her neck. She walks with a limp.

WILSON. She sounds a dear old lady. Where does she normally live? When she's not up half the night careering about visiting?

MIKE. In the suburbs. She prefers it to the city centre.

WILSON. Well, I'm sorry I can't stay. I must be going then. Before I say goodbye would you mind telling me, as briefly as possible, why you killed my brother.

MIKE. I didn't!

WILSON. You did. You were paid two hundred and fifty quid. Exclusive of repairs to the van.

MIKE. No!

WILSON. It was on October the twenty-first he was killed. What were you doing that day?

MIKE. I was fishing.

WILSON. Where?

MIKE. In the canal.

WILSON. Did you catch much?

MIKE. I put it back. That's the rules. The rules of the club.

WILSON. My brother belonged to the club. He was the best angler you had. He gave out the cards. (*Pause.*) What did you catch on the day he died?

MIKE. I can't be expected to remember.

WILSON. Did you have the good fortune to find a salmon on the end of your line?

MIKE. No. Whoever heard of catching salmon in a canal?

WILSON. You killed my brother. Your denials fall on deaf ears. (*Pause.*) You're a liar. That's what it amounts to.

MIKE (*frightened*). What are you going to do?

WILSON. Nothing I can do, is there? (*He picks up his suitcase*

and goes to the door.) I'll be off. (*He smiles, deliberately.*)
Give my love to Maddy.

MIKE. Let me alone. I'm ill. (*Pause.*) What did you say?

WILSON. Maddy. Your old scrubber.

MIKE *goes over to* WILSON

MIKE. Are you asking for a back-hander? What is this about
Maddy? I don't know any Maddy.

WILSON. She lives here.

MIKE. Her name's Joyce.

WILSON *shrugs, smiling.*

Out you go, you young whore's get!

WILSON *smiles.*

Piss off! Coming here trying to make trouble. I was
handy with my fists once. I could make pulp of you.

WILSON. All this energy. Nearly blowing your top. You ought
to get it regular. You'd feel better then.

MIKE. Don't come to me with your gutter talk. I won't listen
to it.

WILSON. You won't have been capable of a jump since the
Festival. It's the usual story.

MIKE *grabs* WILSON'S *arm.*

MIKE. Why did you call her Maddy?

WILSON. She asked me to. In private. It's her trade
name.

MIKE. She never saw you till two days ago.

WILSON. She told you that? Do you believe her?

MIKE. Yes.

WILSON. It's your affair. I never believe a woman. I've had
experience.

MIKE. The only experience you've had is with your fist.

WILSON. What a coarse remark. How typical. (*He glances to
the bedroom.*) I wish she'd change the sheets on the bed.
Have you noticed? It's a bad sign.

MIKE. If you've had her I'll swing for you.

WILSON. Would you kill me?

MIKE. I would. I'd throttle you with my bare hands. I'd choke the filth out of you.

WILSON. You've got a gun. Kill me with that. (*Pause.*) I'll be back tomorrow. Tell Maddy I'll see her.

MIKE. You can believe me. I never murdered your brother. Don't you believe me?

WILSON. No. (*Pause.*) I might decide to put Maddy in the pudding club. Just to show my contempt for your way of life. I never take precautions. We're skin to skin. Nature's method.

> MIKE *gives a groan of pain. He runs to the drawer, rummages and takes the gun from the drawer.*

MIKE (*waving the gun before* WILSON). See this? I'll use it if I catch you with her.

WILSON. How good a shot are you?

MIKE. I'm an expert.

WILSON. The heart is situated . . . (*He points.*) . . . just below this badge on my pullover. Don't miss, will you? I don't want to be injured. I want to be dead.

MIKE. You think I'm joking?

WILSON. I hope you're not.

MIKE. You're an ignorant young sod! Like your brother. It must run in the family.

WILSON. Have you noticed that mole she has?

MIKE. Where?

WILSON. In a private place. I don't expect you've looked lately. That's why she's gone for someone younger.

MIKE (*screaming*). Get out!

> WILSON *smiles and exits.*

(*Softly*). I feel bad. I'm sickening for something.

> *He puts the gun away in the drawer.*

They think because you're a criminal they can treat you like dirt. Coming here like that. Telling a man to his face. The morals of Nineveh were hardly so lax.

> *He sits at the table closing his eyes.*

Oh, but he's playing with fire. I'll shoot him. I'll geld him.
I've a clear case. I'm the injured party. I'll have the stones
off him if he's done her. (*Pause.*) He'll be putting her into
a whorehouse next. These kids have only one idea.

*He goes into the bedroom, picks up his pyjamas and slippers,
pulls the clothing and a pillow from the bed and enters the
main room.*

I'll sleep out here. I can't have her next to me.

He sits on the settee and begins to undress.

Oh, oh! I'm cuckolded. What a spectacle. Yet you'd swear
you were safe with her. She's not much of a looker. The sex
is rotten. Perfidious. Treacherous. She's old enough to be
his mother. (*Pause.*) I shouldn't say that. That's a terrible
thing to say.

He puts on his pyjama jacket.

She's whored herself under two assumed names. Before I
met her she was known to the Directory of Directors as
Madelein Scott-Palmer. And before that she'd led a loose
life as Sarah Fielding. She wasted her auntie's legacy on
cards for tobacconists' windows. Oh, it's too much! I'll have
to kill her.

He puts on his pyjama trousers.

If I kill her I'll have to say goodbye. I'll never see her again.
I'd be alone. The pain of it. I never realise the pain. I'm
too old to start again. Too old. I love her. My heart aches
to admit it. She's all I've got. I want her if she's the biggest
old tart since the mother of Solomon.

He puts on his slippers.

What a life it is living in a country full of whores and
communists.

He puts his coat on as a dressing-gown. JOYCE *enters. She
takes off her cardigan.*

JOYCE. Has he gone?

MIKE (*looking up, narrowing his eyes*). What d'you mean?

JOYCE. I thought he was staying here.

MIKE. Do you want him to?

JOYCE. Do I want him to?

MIKE (*nodding his head*). I see your plan. I see it. You've the cunning of Luther.

> JOYCE *walks past him into the bedroom.*

Where are you going?

JOYCE. To bed. I'm not listening to you.

MIKE. What's she up to? (*Pause.*) I'll maybe forgive her. Our Lord forgave the woman taken in adultery. But the circumstances were different. (*Pause.*) It's a ludicrous business. Ludicrous. The deceit. At her age. She wants somebody younger. At her age they get the itch. It's like a tale told by a commercial traveller. Just for a few minutes' thrill. I don't know what she'd be like if we had a television.

JOYCE (*undressing for bed*). Are you giving a recitation out there?

MIKE (*entering bedroom*). What?

JOYCE. I thought you were entertaining the troops.

MIKE. I leave that to you. That's more your line, isn't it?

JOYCE. What's the matter?

MIKE. You cow! Playing me up.

JOYCE. You shouldn't've invited him in. You upset me.

MIKE. I've heard about you. You'll be taking your clothes off in the street next.

JOYCE. What's got into you?

MIKE. Some men would kill you. You're lucky I'm not some. A fine family. Your mother was doing it in a doorway the night she was killed. If she hadn't been such a wicked old brass she'd've been in the shelter with the rest. Taking the A.R.P. from their duty. Your granny spent Mafeking night on her back. That makes three generations of whores.

> He smacks her face. JOYCE *shrieks with surprise and fright.*

I'll murder you!

> He leaps upon her. They fall across the bed.

JOYCE (*shouting*). Mind the fish! You'll upset my goldfish.

MIKE (*standing up, taking off his coat*). What d'you want to keep fish in a bedroom for? It's not hygienic.

He gets into bed. JOYCE *fetches the pillow and blanket from the main room and puts them on the bed.*

JOYCE. What's he been telling you?

MIKE. Did you let him?

JOYCE (*indignantly*). He never touched me.

MIKE. You'd have to say that. I don't want to lose you. I don't want to be on my own again. I was so lonely before.

JOYCE. Shall I put your coat on your feet? It's freezing again.

SCENE FIVE

Next morning.

JOYCE *is washing dishes. The doorbell rings.* JOYCE *takes off her gloves and wipes her hands. The door is pushed open and* WILSON *enters.*

JOYCE. What are you doing in here? That door is supposed to be locked.

WILSON. There's no lock.

JOYCE. My husband is downstairs. It's true. This time it's true.

WILSON. I know. I saw him hanging about down there. I told him we were having an affair last night. It didn't inconvenience you in any way?

He takes off his coat and spreads it on the settee.

You don't want to have an affair with me by any chance?

JOYCE. You're only a little boy.

WILSON *picks up a chair and wedges it under the handle of the door.*

What are you doing that for?

WILSON. So as when he comes up and tries the handle he'll think we're knocking it off.

JOYCE (*with distaste*). Don't use expressions like that. I'm not used to it.

WILSON. When you were on the game you must've been.

JOYCE. I never allowed anyone to take liberties with me. My people were good class. (*Pause.*) Who told you about me?

WILSON. My brother. He had it off with you after seeing *The Sound of Music*. I waited downstairs. He was as pissed as a fart. He would never have had a prostitute and seen *The Sound of Music* otherwise. (*Loosens his tie.*) You're like most women. Here today and gone tomorrow. My brother's fiancée resembled you in many ways. Fickle in her emotions. She was trying on her wedding-gown when we got news of Frank's death. Now she's had it dyed ice-blue and wears it to dinner dances. My only consolation is that she looks hideous in it. But it shows what kind of woman she is, doesn't it? I knew the type by the way she moved her knees up against my thighs at the funeral. I felt like throttling her. A whole hour she was at it. We went the long way round to avoid the procession.

JOYCE. What procession?

WILSON. They were celebrating some victory or other. We heard the bands playing in the distance. The Royal Family were out in full force. Furs and garters flying. My old man was in it. He couldn't come to the funeral because he was on the British Legion float. He represented something.

He sits, his shoulders hunched, staring into space.

He thought more of tarting himself up than burying his son. All our family seem to be some kind of idiot. If anybody so much as mentions the British Legion to my dad he goes into a trance. On armistice day he takes part in all the rituals. He eats poppies for a week beforehand. I haven't seen him since the funeral. I expect he's in a home by now.

He stands.

He should be up here.

JOYCE. Who?

WILSON. Your old man. We should have some warmth. Haven't you got an electric fire? I hadn't anticipated being frozen to death.

He goes off into the bedroom.

WILSON (*calling from the bedroom*). Are these some kind of carp?

JOYCE. No. Just goldfish.

WILSON enters the main room.

WILSON. You can catch germs from them, you know.

He takes off his tie.

My brother would've been twenty-four in three days' time. He had plans for a business.

He kicks off his shoes.

I expect he would have made good sooner or later. He was the go-ahead type. His mentality was fully developed. He used to read a lot about expansion. His death put a stop to that. I don't take after him. Except in the physical sense.

He sighs and shakes his head.

I get a bit lost without him, I don't mind admitting. (*Pause.*) He might have made a lot of money in his own line. It was my ambition to become the brother of a millionaire. (*Pause.*) I expect you're bored. You didn't know him. I can't expect you to see my point of view.

He takes his pullover off, unbuttons his shirt, pins a badge on his shirt above the heart, and unzips his fly.

JOYCE. Here, what are you doing?

WILSON. It ought to look as if we're on the job when he comes up.

JOYCE. Stop it! Stop it! Whatever will Michael think? He'll think we're carrying on. I never thought of that.

WILSON. I banked on him being up here by now. Rattling the door. He's probably gone back on his word.

He goes into the bedroom and looks out of the window.

He's not out there now.

JOYCE picks up his pullover and goes into the bedroom.

JOYCE (*handing him his pullover*). Put your clothes on. Don't be so silly.

WILSON (*accepting the pullover*). He won't come up. He won't. I can see this is a failure like everything else.

MIKE is heard coming up the stairs.

MIKE. Joycie! Joycie . . .

WILSON. I'm sorry if I've caused trouble. I'm not usually like this. My heart is breaking. I wish I'd been with him when he died.

JOYCE. You poor boy. Oh, you poor boy.

She kisses his cheek tenderly. He holds her close. MIKE *crashes into the room. He advances slowly. Pause.* WILSON *turns from* JOYCE, *smiles at* MIKE, *and zips up his fly.* MIKE *fires the gun.*

The shot crashes into the goldfish bowl. JOYCE *screams. A second shot hits* WILSON *in the chest.*

WILSON. He's shot me.

He crashes to the floor on his knees.

My will is in my overcoat pocket. My address in my pocket diary. Remember will you?

JOYCE (*to* MIKE). What've you done?

WILSON. He took it serious. How charming. (*He coughs, blood spurts from his mouth.*) He's a bit of a nutter if you ask me. Am I dying? I think . . . Oh . . .

He falls forward. Silence.

JOYCE. He's fainted.

MIKE (*laying the gun aside*). He's dead.

JOYCE. But he can't be. You haven't killed him?

MIKE. Bring a sheet. Cover his body.

JOYCE. I've a bit of sacking somewhere.

MIKE. I said a sheet! Give him the best.

He goes into the bedroom and drags a sheet from the bed which he puts over WILSON'S *body.*

JOYCE. What excuse was there to shoot him?

MIKE. He was misbehaving himself with my wife.

JOYCE. But I'm not your wife. And he wasn't.

MIKE. He called you Maddy.

JOYCE. Somebody must've told him about my past. You know what people are. (*Pause.*) Did you have anything to do with his brother's death?

MIKE. Yes.

JOYCE. This is what comes of having no regular job. (*Pause.*) Is the phone box working by the Nag's Head?

MIKE. Yes.

JOYCE. Go to the telephone box. Dial 999. I'll tell them I was assaulted.

MIKE (*horrified*). It'll be in the papers.

JOYCE. Well, perhaps not assaulted. Not completely. You came in just in time.

MIKE. You'll stick by me, Joycie?

JOYCE. Of course, dear. (*She kisses him.*) I love you.
   She sees the shattered goldfish bowl.
   Oh, look Michael! (*Bursting into tears.*) My goldfish!
   She picks up a fish.

MIKE. One of the bullets must've hit the bowl.

JOYCE. They're dead. Poor things. And I reared them so carefully. And while all this was going on they died.
   She sobs. MIKE *puts his arm round her and leads her to the settee. She sits.*

MIKE. Sit down. I'll fetch the police. This has been a crime of passion. They'll understand. They have wives and goldfish of their own.
   JOYCE *is too heartbroken to answer. She buries her face in* MIKE'S *shoulder. He holds her close.*

Curtain

The Erpingham Camp

The Erpingham Camp was produced on television by Rediffusion on 27th June 1966 with the following cast:

ERPINGHAM	.. ..	Reginald Marsh
RILEY	.. ..	Peter Reeves
LOU ..	.. ..	Faith Kent
TED ..	.. ..	Charles Rea
KENNY	.. ..	John Forgeham
EILEEN	.. ..	Angela Pleasence
W. E. HARRISON	.. ..	Peter Honri
JESSIE MASON	.. ..	Avril Fane
PADRE	.. ..	Peter Evans

Directed by James Ormerod

Designed by Frank Nerini

The Erpingham Camp was first staged at the Royal Court Theatre on 6th June 1967 in a double-bill entitled *Crimes of Passion* with the following cast:

ERPINGHAM	Bernard Gallagher
RILEY	Roddy Maude-Roxby
LOU	Pauline Collins
TED	Johnny Wade
EILEEN	Yvonne Antrobus
KENNY	Michael Standing
PADRE	Roger Booth
W. E. HARRISON	Ken Wynne
JESSIE MASON	Josie Bradley
REDCOATS and CAMPERS	Andree Evans
	Rosemary McHale
	Peter John
	Malcolm Reid

Directed by Peter Gill
Designed by Deirdre Clancy

No attempt must be made to reproduce the various locales in a naturalistic manner. A small, permanent set of Erpingham's office is set on a high level. The rest of the stage is an un-localised area. Changes of scene are suggested by lighting and banners after the manner of the Royal Shakespeare Company's productions of Shakespeare's histories.

SCENE ONE

ERPINGHAM'S *office. It is evening.* ERPINGHAM *is seated at his desk.* RILEY *enters and* ERPINGHAM *looks up.*

ERPINGHAM. Where's your badge of office?

RILEY. An oversight, sir. I'm sorry.

ERPINGHAM. You should be wearing your decorations. You know the rules. Any member of the staff found improperly dressed on Saturday night is subject to instant dismissal. Only I am excused.

RILEY. I'll put them on at once.

ERPINGHAM. I didn't make the rules, Chief Redcoat Riley. I only carry them out. Is number four latrine unblocked?

RILEY. Yes.

ERPINGHAM. And the toddlers' paddling pool? Have you removed whatever was causing the disturbance?

RILEY. Yes.

ERPINGHAM. Good. What was it?

RILEY. Two ducks. Made of plastic. They were stuck together.

ERPINGHAM. Beak to beak? (*Pause.*) Was the joinery smutty?

RILEY. Well, sir – the Engineer in charge had to perform surgery.

ERPINGHAM. Did the kiddies see?

RILEY. No. They were having a quick run round with Matron.

ERPINGHAM. I want those ducks destroyed. We've no time for hedonists here. My camp is a pure camp. Give me the report for the day.

RILEY *hands him the report.* ERPINGHAM *glances at it.*

Touching the subject of purity, ask Miss Mason to watch

her language. She's not the only one with heat rash. We all
suffer. I suffer myself. Considerably. Hand me that file, will
you?

   RILEY *gives him the file.* ERPINGHAM *puts the report into
it.*

Has the Padre been released from custody yet?

RILEY. Yes. He's having a lie down. It's been a shattering
experience for him.

ERPINGHAM. It'll be nice to have him back with us again.
I'd like to see him when he's rested.

RILEY. Yes, sir. (*He twists his hands together nervously:
swallowing hard.*) Sir . . .

ERPINGHAM. What?

RILEY. Who will organise the Entertainments tonight?

ERPINGHAM. That's been taken care of. Don't worry. Let
me do the worrying. My shoulders are broad.

RILEY. Should the Organiser not arrive, sir, would you
consider giving me a chance?

ERPINGHAM (*without a second thought*). No.

RILEY. I've the personality. Before I came to you I was Ring-
master for Flanegan's Travelling Circus. We did every port
in Eire. When we played before the Brothers of St Vincent
of Paul a Papal Medal was struck. (*Pause.*) You'll not find
a harder audience than monks.

   ERPINGHAM *sighs. He puts the file away, opens the desk,
takes out a bottle and pours himself a drink.*

ERPINGHAM. You couldn't organise your own backside, Chief
Redcoat Riley. Chances I've given you. Look at the Mother
and Child competition. Disastrous. (*He sips his drink.*)
Ugliest woman competition. You nearly won that yourself.
Causing scandal. Oh, no. You can't possibly be considered
for the job. I'm sorry to cause you disappointment. But there
it is.

   He sips his drink. Pause.

Pick up that flag I've dropped, will you.

RILEY *picks a paper flag from the floor.*

Put it where you'd like a new camp founded.

He turns to a map of the world hanging behind the desk.

Go on. Anywhere on the map. I might even name the new camp after you.

RILEY *sticks the flag into the map.*

(ERPINGHAM, *staring hard, shakes his head.*) You're not cut out to be a pioneer, Riley. Dagenham is already over-developed.

He takes the flag and pins it into the map.

There. That's the place for a new Holiday Centre.

RILEY *looks hard at the map.*

RILEY. It's National Trust territory, sir. There's a bird sanctuary nearby.

ERPINGHAM. Human beings need sanctuaries, Riley, as well as birds. The world is in danger of forgetting the fact. Open my drawer. Take out my personal file.

RILEY *opens the drawer and takes out a heavy folder.*

(ERPINGHAM *flicks open the file.*) I shall be a millionaire by the 'seventies.

RILEY. I'll take you up on it.

ERPINGHAM. Make a note if you like.

He lights a cigar, blows a cloud of smoke into the air, smiles, and gives an expansive wave of his hand.

Rows of Entertainment Centres down lovely, unspoiled bits of the coast, across deserted moorland and barren mountainside. The Earthly Paradise. Ah . . .

He stares raptly into the distance.

I can hear it. I can touch it. And the sight of it is hauntingly beautiful, Riley.

Music: 'The Holy City'.

There'll be dancing. And music. Colourful scenes. Official pageantry. Trained drum Majorettes will march hourly across the greensward. The shapeliest girls in Britain – picked from thousands of disappointed applicants. There'll be no shortage of horses. And heated pools. The accommodation will be lavish. Slot-machines will be employed for all tasks. They'll come from far and wide to stay at my entertainment centres. The great ones of this world and, if Fame's trumpet blows long and hard enough, of the next.

The music fades. ERPINGHAM *sinks back, shaking his head.* The Vision that delighted has gone. But – in a short time – I'll have it here. (*He bangs the folder.*) In black and white.

He puts the folder away. RILEY *shakes his head.*

RILEY. Oh, take care, sir. One flick of Fortune's wheel and you'll be brought low. I was taught by a nun once who itched like the Devil to become Superior. One day the message came from the Eternal City. Sister Mary had made it. Promoted to Higher Office. She was overjoyed. But – God's anger light upon me if I'm not telling the truth – as they sang the Te Deum she was seized in a sudden fit and fell to the ground mouthing something that nobody understood – save an old lay sister who'd once been an usherette at the Roxy and was more worldly than the rest. Sister Mary had got to be Superior, but she had to be put away for her foolish pride in believing she had it all worked out. So, take care, sir. I know too well what the punishment is for your kind of sin. It's written over and over again in the books of the Ancient East. And in the Bible too.

ERPINGHAM *swallows the last of his whisky.*

ERPINGHAM. We live in a rational world, Riley. I've no use for your Hibernian cant.

The telephone rings. ERPINGHAM *answers it.*

Good. I'll send someone down. (*He puts the phone down.*) The Entertainments Organiser has arrived. Go and welcome him.

RILEY *goes off.*

SCENE TWO

A chalet. LOU *and* TED *are dressing.*

LOU. I've invited a young couple over. I gave her some help in the salad queue. We don't have to see them again if we don't get on.

The loudspeaker crackles and ERPINGHAM'S *voice is heard.*

ERPINGHAM. Good evening, Ladies and Gentlemen. I've one or two announcements to make.

TED puts on his coat. LOU *brushes him down.*

The Glamorous Granny competition was won by Mrs Anthea Wong of Gresham Road, London, E.17.

LOU. That Chinese woman. See, I told you she'd win.

TED. They marry so young. Seems hardly fair on ordinary people.

ERPINGHAM. The Mother and Child competition resulted in a dead heat. Mrs J. M. Nash of Palmers Green and Mrs Susanne Mitchel of Southampton both win cash prizes.

TED. That fair woman who entered with the dog got nowhere then?

LOU puts the brush away.

ERPINGHAM. Our disability bonus was won by Mr Laurie Russel of Market Harborough. Both Laurie's legs were certified 'absolutely useless' by our Resident Medical Officer. Yet he performed the Twist and the Bossa Nova to the tune specified on the entrance form.

TED. He fell over, though. Twice.

LOU. They help them a lot, don't they? That blind woman would've never found the diving-board if the audience hadn't shouted out.

ERPINGHAM. There are a number of lost children awaiting collection. Would you check your family? A Jewish ex-serviceman is at this moment telling of his experiences both during and after the Nazis' rise to power. In the Number Two dining hall. Admission free.

There is knocking at the chalet door.

All holidaymakers intending taking part in our evening routine should report in person with your numbered card to the Grand Ballroom at eight sharp. Thank you, Ladies and Gentlemen.

LOU *opens the chalet door, and cries loudly.*

LOU. It's Kenny and Eileen! Come in!

KENNY *and* EILEEN *enter, smiling.*

EILEEN. Hope we're not too early?

LOU. No. We're just finishing. This is my husband, Ted. Ted, this is Kenny and Eileen.

There are smiles and handshakes. EILEEN *gives a cry of surprise.*

EILEEN. Oh, Louie! What lovely glasses. I've always wanted a pair like that.

LOU. Why don't you get a pair?

EILEEN. My eyes aren't bad enough. (*She sits beside* KENNY.) And I can't take risks. I'm pregnant, you see.

KENNY. It's our first. (*He smiles, taking* EILEEN *by the hand.*) Not our last, though, eh? (*He kisses her cheek.*) We've only been married a year. We had trouble.

EILEEN. We were banned. I had a breakdown over it. We were so much in love, see.

She snuggles up against KENNY.

KENNY. Her parents caused trouble. We met at a club. We knew we were made for each other from the first moment. It was persuading her parents to see our point of view. That was the most urgent problem. Her father was stubborn, very much of his own frame of mind. Her mother sided with him, naturally. I was at my wits end to find a solution. In the end I bashed them both about the ear. And after that we had no trouble.

EILEEN. We're content now. We're expecting our first child. We have to give up luxuries. Chief among them not going abroad for the sun.

TED puts his hand over LOU's.

TED. Lou and I don't have to bother with that sort of thing.

LOU (*smiling*). We've our sun-lamp, you see.

Pause. Awkward smiles. Pause.

TED. It's interesting you meeting your wife at a club, Ken. I met my wife outside the Young Conservatives.

LOU. I've always found them polite and sympathetic people. I used to spend an hour or two there every Thursday and Saturday. I met the daughter of a brain-specialist on one occasion. She was playing table-tennis and she asked me if I'd act as scorer. Of course, you get your snobs there, same as anywhere else. But on the whole, I enjoyed myself.

TED. Yes. It was outside the Young Conservative Club that I met my fate.

Laughter. Pause.

KENNY. I never liked the Tories 'cause I suspected they weren't decent.

TED frowns.

TED. What d'you mean?

KENNY. Well – look how they carry on. (*Laughing it off.*) They are the 'blue' party, aren't they?

Silence.

TED. It's clear, if you don't mind me saying so, Kenneth, that you've no real knowledge of the English political scene. Your Labour party scandals have increased considerably of latter years.

KENNY. I'm not a Labour man!

LOU and TED smile.

TED. I thought you were.

KENNY. I keep away from all that. I owe it to Eileen.

EILEEN. I'm expecting.

TED (*laughing lightly*). Our Socialist friends would stop you doing that. They'd ban it.

EILEEN. Our love was banned.

KENNY. I knocked her dad's teeth in. I can't stand intolerance.

EILEEN. We're saving up to buy a house.

LOU *smiles*.

LOU. We were left our house. There was never any question of paying for it.

EILEEN *colours pink*.

EILEEN. We've no use for that sort of thing. We don't agree with it.

LOU. You can't go all the way with that kind of philosophy, Eileen. You've got to face facts.

EILEEN. I was brought up to think different. (*Her voice rising.*) My mum was on a lecture once. She could tell you a thing or two. They exhibited her as a reference. My dad was with her. And although they got our love forbidden and made life not worth living, I'm pregnant now and they've been good parents. I can't accept what you say, Louie. It seems wrong to me.

    She bursts into tears. KENNY *comforts her.* LOU *and* TED *stand.*

LOU (*at last, brightly*). I think it's time we joined the festivities.

    EILEEN *dries her tears.*

SCENE THREE

ERPINGHAM'S *office.* RILEY *enters.*

RILEY. Oh, sir! Disaster has struck.

ERPINGHAM. Has the Padre been up to his tricks again?

RILEY. The Entertainments Organiser has been taken bad.

ERPINGHAM. Is he drunk?

RILEY. We don't know. It's a mysterious affliction that's come upon him.

ERPINGHAM. Where is he?

RILEY. In the Hospital Tent, sir. The Resident Medical Officer has given him up for lost.

W. E. HARRISON enters.

W. E. HARRISON. Sir! The Entertainments Organiser has been shown the four last things. The Padre is with him.

The PADRE enters.

PADRE. Sir! The Entertainments Organiser is dead.

ERPINGHAM (*to* RILEY). Remind me to send one of our Class A (Highest Employee) wreaths to his next of kin.

RILEY. Yes, sir.

ERPINGHAM turns sharply to W. E. HARRISON.

ERPINGHAM. Why aren't you in the Music Room, W. E. Harrison?

W. E. HARRISON. My partner, Miss Mason, is doing her solo number, sir.

ERPINGHAM. She can't manage on her own. Go and help her.

W. E. HARRISON goes off.

ERPINGHAM. Did you see this thing happen, Riley?

RILEY. Yes, sir. He was a grand chap, it seems. He'd many original ideas on mass entertainment. I was lapping it up – seeing as I'm ambitious. I made a few notes and was about to question him further when, without a word of warning, he slumps forward in his chair. God help us all, I thought to myself, though I didn't breathe the worst of it out loud, he's been done in.

ERPINGHAM (*to the* PADRE). Had he any enemies?

PADRE. We'd no time to ascertain, sir, before he lost consciousness.

ERPINGHAM gives RILEY a shrewd, hard look.

ERPINGHAM. Did you murder him, Chief Redcoat Riley?

RILEY. No.

ERPINGHAM. We can't have members of the staff taking

human life. We're not equipped to deal with such a situation. Consult the manual. You'll find funerals are frowned upon.

RILEY. He was struck down by something unknown to medical science.

ERPINGHAM. I shall have to take your word for it, Chief Redcoat Riley. Though you're a notorious liar.

RILEY *twists his fingers together in great excitement.*

RILEY. Sir – who will organise the entertainments tonight? We must make a quick decision. The campers are gathering under the bunting.

ERPINGHAM *chews his lip.* RILEY *holds his breath.*

ERPINGHAM. I'll be magnanimous, Riley, and give you the chance of a lifetime. Seize it with both hands.

ERPINGHAM *takes a box from the desk and hands it to the* PADRE. *The* PADRE *takes a sash from the box which he hands to* ERPINGHAM. RILEY *bows his head.* ERPINGHAM *puts the sash upon him.* ERPINGHAM *lifts another box and hands it to the* PADRE. *The* PADRE *opens it, removes a badge and pins it upon* RILEY's *blazer.* RILEY *is bathed in an unearthly radiance.*

Music: 'Zadok the Priest and Nathan the Prophet Anointed Solomon King'.

ERPINGHAM *embraces* RILEY.

ERPINGHAM. Serve us well, Chief Redcoat Riley. And my best wishes for the task ahead.

Music: 'Land of Hope and Glory'.

Your reward will be the heartfelt thanks of the whole of our community. Tonight is your testing time. Let the spirit of Enterprise and Achievement go with you. Remember our Glorious Dead. How many soldiers have had tasks like yours? And carried them through – though their lives were forfeit. The courage and grit that founded Empires still stands. And when, Riley, we plant our first flag upon the white, untouched plains of Asia – you will be in our thoughts that day. The Camps of India, the Eternal Tents of the East will echo to your name as we remember the deed with which you won your spurs. And in those times we shall rejoice that, of your own free will, you were born an Englishman.

The music fades.

RILEY. I was born in County Mayo, sir.

ERPINGHAM. Ireland counts as England.

RILEY. Not with the Irish, sir.

ERPINGHAM. It's England you're representing in the Great Fight. Ireland has empty roads, Galway Bay and the remains of Sir Roger Casement. Isn't that enough?

RILEY. More than enough, sir. We'd be a nation of poets and talkers still with only two of them.

ERPINGHAM *shakes him by the hand.*

ERPINGHAM. Good luck then. Away with you.

PADRE. Take God's blessing with you, my son. And remember always to keep the little text I gave you. The words are obscure but the picture will keep you from harm.

RILEY. Thank you, Father. And thank you, sir. I shall prove myself worthy. Goodbye.

He turns and goes off. ERPINGHAM *takes off his coat.*

ERPINGHAM. I'm going to undress, Padre. Cover up the portrait of Her Majesty.

The PADRE *covers over the large framed portrait of the Queen on the desk.* ERPINGHAM *strips down to his underwear.*

ERPINGHAM. Have you prepared your sermon for tomorrow?

PADRE. Yes, sir.

ERPINGHAM. Is it fit to be preached?

PADRE. I hope you'll give me any cuts that may be necessary, sir.

ERPINGHAM. What is the subject?

PADRE. The Miracles of Jesus.

ERPINGHAM. I hope we're not in for some far-fetched tale set among the Bedouin?

He hands his clothes to the PADRE *who goes off.*

ERPINGHAM *takes a pair of corsets from a drawer in the desk. The* PADRE *returns with a dress suit and shirt on a hanger. He lays them on the desk.* EPPINGHAM *puts on the corset.*

PADRE. I intend to deal with the meaning of the Gadarene demoniac. I shall draw one or two conclusions that may surprise you, sir.

ERPINGHAM. I don't go to Church on Sunday morning to be surprised, Padre. Lace me up, will you?

The PADRE *laces up* ERPINGHAM's *corset.* ERPINGHAM *lifts his leg. The* PADRE *fastens* ERPINGHAM's *suspenders and laces* ERPINGHAM's *shoes.*

PADRE. I wonder, sir, whether you've ever stopped to consider the meaning of the Gadarene swine?

ERPINGHAM. I haven't, Padre. Hand me my shirt.

The PADRE *hands* ERPINGHAM *his shirt and* ERPINGHAM *puts it on.*

PADRE. You recall, sir, how a madman was cured of his delusions. How the devils within him took up abode in a herd of swine? How the swine ran mad causing great destruction?

He hands ERPINGHAM *his trousers and* ERPINGHAM *puts them on.*

ERPINGHAM. It's a most instructive tale. What meaning do you attach to it?

PADRE. We are meant to understand, sir, that with madness, as with vomit, it's the passer-by who receives the inconvenience.

ERPINGHAM. If Christianity had been as powerful as your similes, Padre, it would've conquered the world. Pass my tie.

The PADRE *passes him the tie.*

SCENE FOUR

RILEY *and* JESSIE MASON.

MASON. I'll make the announcement, Chief Redcoat Riley. And then, to follow, I suggest my juggling act. You may remember it proved extremely popular at Catlin's Arcadia last summer?

RILEY. Just make the announcement. Leave the rest to me.

MASON. The public appreciate a highly skilled performer. Nobody remains unimpressed by the sheer professionalism I bring to my act.

RILEY. Just cue me in. That's all I require.

JESSIE MASON *tosses her head.*

MASON. You're making a big mistake in not taking advantage of my wide experience with the average holiday-maker.

W. E. HARRISON *enters.*

W. E. HARRISON. Everything is ready Chief Redcoat Riley. They're waiting for you in the Grand Ballroom.

RILEY. I'll require you and Mason to assist me with the distribution of prizes. And bring your squeeze-box, Mason. Music is most important in creating a relaxed, informal atmosphere.

He strides off. JESSIE MASON *and* W. E. HARRISON *follow.*

SCENE FIVE

ERPINGHAM'S *office.* ERPINGHAM *has finished dressing.*

ERPINGHAM. You're interested in religion then, Padre?

PADRE. From a purely Christian point of view, sir.

He helps ERPINGHAM *on with his tail-coat and brushes him down.*

I find great solace in the life of the Spirit.

ERPINGHAM. I'm sure you do. (*He turns to allow the* PADRE *to brush his back.*) What happened to you in court this morning?

PADRE. I was acquitted, sir. The young woman withdrew her charge.

ERPINGHAM. I'm pleased to hear it. You must give up your evangelical forays into teenage chalets. They're liable to misinterpretation. Take the blindfold from Her Majesty. I can give her an audience now.

The PADRE *uncovers the Queen's portrait.*

And you'd better find another subject for your sermon tomorrow. I don't feel that the story of the Gadarene swine has any real meaning for us today.

SCENE SIX

RILEY *is in the spotlight onstage in the Grand Ballroom. On either side of him stand* JESSIE MASON *and* W. E. HARRISON. MASON *smiles, archly.* HARRISON, MASON *and the assembled Redcoats sing and dance a medley of songs which includes 'Put on your Ta-Ta Little Girlie', 'Linger a Little Longer', 'In a Little Gypsy Tearoom', 'If I had my Way, Dear, You'd Never Grow Old', and 'Let the Great Big World go Turning'.* JESSIE MASON *accompanies on her concertina.*

MASON. And now, that likeable lad from across the Irish Sea, Chief Redcoat Kevin Riley!

RILEY *steps forward, modestly, yet with a cool, relaxed manner.*

RILEY. I'm in charge of entertainments tonight, Ladies and Gentlemen. And I'm going to see we all have a whale of a time. Tonight is fun night. And, as many of our old campers knows anything can happen on fun night at Camp Erpingham!

JESSIE MASON *plays a chord on her squeeze-box.* W. E. HARRISON *produces two flags and waves them with a gay flourish.* RILEY *beams.*

Who's going to be our 'Tarzan of the Apes' this week?
Who'll volunteer? Come along now. Don't hold back. Don't
spoil the fun. Our friend here (*Nods to* W. E. HARRISON.) has
a prize for the gent who'll volunteer. Now who'll be
'Tarzan'?

> KENNY *steps on to the stage, a little sheepishly.*

KENNY. I'll have a go.

RILEY. Good lad. First a kiss from Jessie Mason, our glamorous songstress! (*Leads* KENNY *to* MASON.) Mind her
squeeze-box now! A fellow from Belfast got his hand caught
in it last week. (*Laughs, beerily.*) They all want to get their
fingers on Miss Mason's squeeze-box!

> MASON *kisses* KENNY. W. E. HARRISON *produces a leopard
> skin with a gay flourish.* MASON *plays a chord.*

(*To* KENNY). I want you to put this on. It's our resident
'Tarzan' gear.

> KENNY *takes the skin and is about to put it on.* RILEY
> *stops him.*

You'll have to drop your slacks, my lad.

> KENNY *looks dubious.* MASON *gives a giggle and a pro-
> fessionally coy smile.*

MASON. He doesn't want to take them off in front of a lady.

RILEY. Where's the lady? You're not trying to tell us that
you're a lady, Miss Mason?

MASON. I am.

RILEY. We'll have to check your credentials later. (*To* KENNY.)
Go with Miss Mason. She plays to the house. You'll have
a whale of a time, but remember to keep your cheques and
your legs crossed!

> KENNY, *with a blush, attempts a joke.*

KENNY. I don't know whether I should do this. I'm a married
man.

RILEY. And Mason is a married woman. She's married to the
Chef. That's how she got on the game!

> MASON *leads* KENNY *off.* W. E. HARRISON *beams.*

RILEY. And while we're waiting I'll sing you a little song I
was taught when I lived near Fermanagh as a youth.

> W. E. HARRISON *accompanies* RILEY *on* MASON's *squeeze-
> box*. RILEY *sings in a nasal Irish tenor*.

'Sure of all the Irish songs I know,
There's one I love the best,
'Tis a symphony of love to me—
'Tis sweeter than the rest.
My melody, my rosary, my tender lullaby
'Tis you I mean,
My sweet Colleen,
And here's the reason why.

Sure you have all the charms of my Mother Machree.
You're my wild Irish rose.
You remind me of a valley,
Where the River Shannon flows.
When your Irish eyes are smiling,
I know where my heart belongs.
You're a little piece of Heaven,
You're my Irish song of songs.

Sure there's music in your pretty smile,
There's music in your eyes.
There's a rhythm too,
In all you do,
That you don't realise.
There seems to be,
A melody,
In everything you say.
When you are near,
I seem to hear
The songs of yesterday.

> *He gathers himself up and finishes with a fine flourish.*

When your Irish eyes are smiling,

I know where my heart belongs,
You're a little piece of Heaven,
You're my Irish song of songs!

As he acknowledges the end of the song, MASON *returns with*
KENNY. *He is dressed in the leopard skin. He looks sheepishly
around.* W. E. HARRISON *plays a frenzied cadenza on the
squeeze-box.* JESSIE MASON *produces two flags and waves
them with a gay flourish.* RILEY *approaches* KENNY.
Magnificent! Really wonderful!

KENNY *flexes his muscles. Everyone looks benevolent.*
You'll have a wonderful week as our resident 'Tarzan
of the Apes'. You'll be called upon to perform many
interesting acts. I'll give you the details later. And now I'd
like two ladies please! Who'll oblige? Come along now,
don't be shy.

EILEEN *and* LOU *step on to the stage.*
Ladies! Have you ever seen a finer specimen of young
manhood? (*He points to* KENNY.) Wouldn't you like to
find that in your 'in tray'?

EILEEN. I often do. (*With a quick giggle.*) He's my husband!
Everyone looks surprised. Laughter.

RILEY. Your husband, eh? Well, you almost lost him to
Jessie Mason our resident nymphomaniac!

EILEEN *pouts and pretends, rather archly, to be indifferent.*

EILEEN. She can have him if she fancies him. He's no good to
me!

RILEY. No good to you, eh? (*With a look at* EILEEN's *pregnant
belly.*) It looks as though you've been good to him, though?
Eh?

Everybody laughs. EILEEN *blushes.* W. E. HARRISON *hands
the squeeze-box to* MASON.

(*To* EILEEN *and* LOU). Who's going to scream the loudest?
Loudest scream wins a cash prize. Just scream. As loud
as you like! The winner will be given a voucher for

the Erpingham Stores. A voucher that will enable you to buy a week's groceries or, if you prefer, three days' luxuries, free of charge. Who's going to scream?

JESSIE MASON *plays a few chords and a flourish on the squeeze-box.* W. E. HARRISON *produces two flags and waves them with a gay smile.*

(*To* LOU). All you've got to do is scream!

LOU *begins to scream, but stops suddenly.*

(*To* EILEEN). All you've got to do is scream!

EILEEN *screams and stops, then screams again. She gives a giggle.* LOU *screams, louder this time.* KENNY, *losing his shyness, flexes his muscles and walks around* MASON *like an ape.* MASON *smiles.* LOU *and* EILEEN *are now screaming loudly.*

One more gentleman? Who else is game?

TED *runs on to the stage.*

Take your clothes off, sir. I'd like you to do the can-can. *Needing no more persuading* TED *takes off his trousers and coat and, to the tune of the can-can from 'Orpheus in the Underworld' played on* MASON's *squeeze-box, he dances a can-can with his shirt tails flying.*

Oh, wonderful, wonderful! We're going to have a lovely time, Ladies and Gentlemen! A gorgeous time!

LOU *and* EILEEN *are screaming,* KENNY *is grunting and grinning like an ape, and flexing his muscles at an indifferent* MASON. TED *is dancing the can-can, whilst* MASON *plays the squeeze-box.* W. E. HARRISON *produces flags and waves them with a gay flourish.*

(*To* LOU *and* EILEEN). All right now! O.K.! That's enough of it. I'll judge the loudest scream now.

The two women continue to scream loudly and hysterically. He puts his hand on EILEEN's *shoulder, and drags her away from* LOU.

O.K.! (EILEEN *screams and weeps.*) Oh, God! She's hysterical. (*To* EILEEN.) Stop it, will you?

EILEEN *clings to him. He pushes her away and slaps her face.* EILEEN *collapses into hysterical sobbing. There is a loud shout from* KENNY *and* LOU *abruptly stops screaming.* KENNY *hurries over to* EILEEN.

KENNY. What did you do to her?

RILEY (*backing away from him*). I smacked her face. She was becoming hysterical.

KENNY. Is that your idea of a joke? Ask a woman to scream and then smack her in the mouth?

RILEY *draws himself up to his full height.*

RILEY. Get back to your place. There's been a misunderstanding.

KENNY. Hit a pregnant woman? You pig!

EILEEN *weeps.*

EILEEN. He hit me! I'm an expectant mother!

KENNY *knocks* RILEY *to the floor with a blow to the mouth. He falls upon him, and* EILEEN *dances over them screaming.* Hit him! Hit him!

Seeing what is happening, LOU *screams with fright and attempts to part the two men.* TED *is still dancing. Oblivious to the scene in front of them,* JESSIE MASON *is playing the squeeze-box and* W. E. HARRISON, *with a beaming smile, produces flags at intervals and waves them with a gay flourish. At last* MASON *becomes aware that something has gone wrong. She stops playing and stares, open-mouthed.*

MASON. Here! You weren't asked to do that. (*To* EILEEN.) Make him stop!

TED, *who has been dancing involuntarily without* MASON'S *music, stops and ambles over with a cheeky expression.*

TED. When do we collect our prizes?

RILEY *staggers to his feet and wipes his nose with the back of his hand.*

RILEY. Get off the stage! You've forfeited your prizes.

TED, *upset, turns away and stares about him, puzzled.*

KENNY *seizes* RILEY *by the lapels.*

KENNY. I'm having an apology out of you! Call yourself a man? Hitting a pregnant woman!

> EILEEN *weeps, occasionally she says* 'Why don't you thump him one?' *or* 'He hit me, Ken'.

TED (*to* LOU). My trousers! Somebody's nicked my trousers!

> LOU *gives a cry of distress. She goes to* RILEY.

LOU. My husband's trousers have been stolen! We shall hold you responsible for their loss.

> W. E. HARRISON *looks on with a beaming smile and waves his flags with a gay flourish. He winks at* MASON.

W. E. HARRISON. Chief Redcoat Riley has earned his money tonight, Jes. Why, he's got them eating out of his hand.

> *There is a sudden cry of pain from* RILEY, *accompanied by shouts of rage from* KENNY, *hysterical sobbing from* EILEEN *and indignant bellows of* 'My husband has had his trousers stolen!' *from* LOU. TED *is wandering about the stage searching.*

MASON (*frigidly to* W. E. HARRISON). This is what you can expect when you're not an experienced all-round family entertainer. Go and tell Mr Erpingham what's happened.

> W. E. HARRISON *gives her a look of pained surprise and hurries away.* MASON *comes downstage and, with the screaming and arguing campers behind her, smiles brightly and begins to play and sing* 'Fold Your Wings of Love Around Me'.

SCENE SEVEN

> ERPINGHAM'S *office.* ERPINGHAM *is now fully dressed in white tie and tails. A noise of screaming is heard in the distance mingled with music and excited shouts.*

ERPINGHAM (*smoothing his hair with a brush*). I'd like your presence at the bathing beauty contest tomorrow, Padre.

A clerical face always inspires confidence at a gathering of semi-nude women. (*He puts the brush down.*) And, in the evening, perhaps you'd mingle with the older men and tell a few of your 'off-colour' stories?

PADRE. I'll make a note in my diary, sir.

He does so.

ERPINGHAM. Bearing in mind the large number of Roman Catholic guests we have this week it might be wise not to include the one about the Pope's mother-in-law.

The distant noise rises sharply.

Can you hear anything?

PADRE. I was aware of a growing tumult, sir. It's coming from the Grand Ballroom.

ERPINGHAM. It sounds like the Devil's Mass.

W. E. HARRISON enters. He is dishevelled and out of breath.

W. E. HARRISON. Would you come and cast your eye over the Grand Ballroom, sir?

ERPINGHAM. Why? What's going on?

W. E. HARRISON. Nothing, sir. Riley's got them a bit over-excited that's all. (*He laughs a little breathlessly.*)

ERPINGHAM. Pass me that gardenia.

The PADRE hands him the gardenia. ERPINGHAM puts it into his buttonhole.

Encouraging them to make that racket. He's exceeding his brief. (*He pins the gardenia on.*) Pass the spray.

W. E. HARRISON passes a scent spray.

What was the row about? Do you know?

W. E. HARRISON. Riley was trying to pacify some young chap's wife, sir. The husband got hold of the wrong end of the stick.

ERPINGHAM sprays the gardenia with scent.

ERPINGHAM. If we have complaints from women I'll see Riley is prosecuted. (*He puts the spray aside.*) Give me a cigar.

W. E. HARRISON hands him a cigar.

Every one of us must behave like Caesar's wife. (*He cuts the cigar.*)

MASON *runs in. She looks pale and shaken. Her dress is torn and her hair is awry. She carries her squeeze-box.*

MASON (*to* ERPINGHAM). Oh, sir! Would you go to the Grand Ballroom? Chief Redcoat Riley is in considerable difficulties. Certain elements in the camp have taken advantage of his inexperience to behave badly. They've broken the mirror at the back of 'non-alcoholic' drinks bar.

ERPINGHAM *turns to the* PADRE *with a frown.*

ERPINGHAM. You see, Padre, I act like a Christian and what happens? Property is damaged, women insulted and the representatives of lawful government frightened out of their wits.

He turns crisply to W. E. HARRISON *and* JESSIE MASON.

I shan't need your help. Run over the menu for dinner. Come with me, Padre. I've made Riley and I'll break him. He'll be reduced to hanging around Irish Labour Rallies. Entertaining the Bishop of Armagh and that crowd.

He sticks the cigar into the corner of his mouth and exits followed by the PADRE. W. E. HARRISON *and* MASON *stand at ease.*

W. E. HARRISON. My nerves will be on the twitch for weeks after this. A grown woman came up and spat in my face.

MASON. Would you recognise her again?

W. E. HARRISON. I wouldn't want to. Gob all over my carnation. Disgusting. I had to flush it down the teenagers toilet. (*He takes a notebook from his pocket.*) Chief Redcoat bloody Riley showed his incompetence tonight all right.

MASON. It went from bad to worse after you left. Some great lout climbed on the stage and tried to take my clothes off! (*With a smile.*) You see, Wally, he'd got a totally false impression of my character. When Riley said I was the resident nympho they took it as gospel. He had his hand up my skirt and my briefs round my ankles before I knew what had happened. Kept shrieking 'Give us a feel of your squeeze-box'. (*With a shrug.*) There should be a distance between the artist and her public. I don't like rowdy behaviour from my fans.

    W. E. HARRISON *opens his note-book.*

W. E. HARRISON. We'll begin the inspection with the cold meats.

    MASON *claps her hands.*
    Music: 'Dead March' from 'Saul'.
    WAITERS *enter slowly pushing a trolley upon which is a variety of cold meats: hams, cold chickens, sausages, a pig's head and trotters. The cortège passes in front of* MASON *and* W. E. HARRISON *who bow their heads. The music fades as the* WAITERS *go off.*

SCENE EIGHT

    ERPINGHAM *and the* PADRE *are walking swiftly to the Grand Ballroom.*

ERPINGHAM. You realise, of course, that Riley's behaviour is a legacy of the potato famine?

PADRE. I'm reminded of Moses on Sinai discovering the excesses of the Children of Israel. Once again the literal truth of the Bible has been demonstrated!

ERPINGHAM. I'd rather you didn't mention these Jewish myths, Padre. I don't know about you, but I'm a Christian.

    RILEY *is seen between two men.* LOU, EILEEN *and several* CAMPERS *stand round him. Many have bleeding faces.* TED *is still without his trousers.* LOU *has wound bunting round herself. She has a distracted air.* KENNY, *still in the leopard skin, holds* RILEY *under the chin. Blood pours from* RILEY'*s mouth and nose.*

KENNY. Apologise, you cowson! Give me an apology!

RILEY *shakes his head; he is hardly conscious.*

EILEEN (*with a shriek*). Hit him again! Give him a good hiding!

    LOU *passes a hand across her brow, dazed. She laughs weakly.*

KENNY. Pregnant women, eh? I'll teach you to hit pregnant women!

    ERPINGHAM *and the* PADRE *advance upon the group in horror.*

ERPINGHAM. Leave that man alone! He's a member of the staff.

    KENNY *smacks* RILEY's *face, first with the flat of his hand, then with the back.*

KENNY. I won't have pregnant women insulted.

ERPINGHAM. Any disciplinary action will be taken by me. You've no right to strike an official of the Camp.

    He tries to thrust KENNY *out of the way. He struggles with* KENNY. LOU *tries to intervene.*

LOU. His wife was insulted.

TED. Carrying she is. She's four months.

ERPINGHAM (*staring at* TED, *outraged*). What has become of your trousers? (*To the* PADRE.) This is no place for a priest. (*Back to* TED.) I don't allow indecent exposure in my camp. Consult the manual. You'll find it in the drawer beside your bed.

    KENNY, *emotionally, appeals to* ERPINGHAM.

KENNY. It's our first child. We've only been married a year. We were refused permission to wed.

EILEEN (*weeping*). We defied the ban on our love! (*She cries hysterically.*) I'm pregnant. I've a right to protection, haven't I?

    LOU *bangs* RILEY *in the groin with her handbag.* RILEY *screams in pain and would collapse if* TED *didn't drag him to his feet.* ERPINGHAM, *extremely angry at the turn of events, tries to push* KENNY *aside and bring* RILEY *to safety.*

KENNY. Hanging's too good for the bleeder!

> ERPINGHAM *gives* KENNY *a shove which sends him spinning. He grabs* RILEY *by the arm.* KENNY *comes back;* EILEEN *hits* ERPINGHAM *on the back of the head with a bottle.* ERPINGHAM *sinks to his knees.*

PADRE (*lifting his hands in horror*). That's Mr Erpingham!

> *He supports* ERPINGHAM *and helps him to rise.*

(*White-faced*). You've struck a figure of authority!

> ERPINGHAM *shakes his head, dizzily. He stands upright, frees himself from the* PADRE *and turns coldly upon* EILEEN.

ERPINGHAM. You are banned from the Erpingham Camp for life!

> EILEEN *makes a farting noise. The rest of the* CAMPERS *jeer. The* PADRE *wrings his hands.*

(*Rounding upon the campers*). All of you return to your chalets! Quick now! I shall make an announcement!

> *There is angry jeering laughter and mocking whistles from* KENNY.

Let's get out of this, Padre. (*He turns to go.*)

PADRE. What about Chief Redcoat Riley, sir?

> TED *releases* RILEY *who drops to the ground in a faint.*

ERPINGHAM. Send the doctor over. The evening has been a complete disaster.

> ERPINGHAM *makes a speedy exit followed by the* PADRE.

SCENE NINE

> W. E. HARRISON *and* JESSIE MASON *are inspecting the food.* MASON *holds a menu.* W. E. HARRISON *has his note-book open.*

W. E. HARRISON. Trifles and assorted savouries.

> MASON *claps her hands.*

Music: 'Chinese Dance' from 'The Nutcracker Suite'.
WAITERS *enter quickly pushing a trolley upon which is a variety of jellies, pastries, trifles and sweets.*

W. E. HARRISON. Taste that trifle, Mason.

MASON *takes a cardboard spoon from the trolley and tastes the trifle.*

MASON. Very good, I'd say.

W. E. HARRISON. Destroy the spoon.

MASON *screws up the spoon and gives it to a waiter.*
WAITERS *push the trolley out of sight. The music fades.*
MASON *looks at the menu.* W. E. HARRISON *writes in his book.*

W. E. HARRISON. Drinks of choice with meal. We'll do them and sign the Chef's report.

ERPINGHAM'*s voice is heard.*

ERPINGHAM. Harrison! Harrison!

ERPINGHAM *enters with the* PADRE. *Both are distressed.*

MASON. Shall we inspect the doilies now or later?

ERPINGHAM. See the Main Gate is locked, Harrison. Bring the keys to me!

HARRISON *goes off.*

MASON (*with a charming smile, in a soothing voice*). We've checked the menu for tonight, sir. It's quite in order. Would you care to sign the Chef's report?

ERPINGHAM. No. (*He tears the menu apart.*) Lock the food away! I'm not feeding that Hellish squadron out there.

MASON *gives a squeak of surprise and alarm.*

MASON. Whatever has happened, sir?

PADRE. It was dreadful. Quite dreadful, Miss Mason. The bunting has been torn down from the Beauty Queen's Parade.

ERPINGHAM. They were running about half-naked spewing up their pork 'n beans. I counted eight pairs of women's briefs on the stairs. There'll be some unexpected visits to the Pre-natal clinic after tonight. (*He mops his brow.*) It

would take the pen of our National poet to describe the
scene that met my eyes upon entering the Grand Ballroom.
My Chief Redcoat was being savagely beaten about the
face by a man dressed as a leopard.

PADRE. It was like an allegorical painting by one of the lesser
Masters. I was forcibly reminded of a 'Christ Mocked'
which was, until recently, hanging in the cellar of the Walker
Art Gallery, Liverpool.

ERPINGHAM. When I remonstrated with them I was sub-
jected to abuse. I was struck upon the head by a bottle. They
were completely out of control.

MASON (*with wonder*). Hit an official of the Camp? That's
never been done before.

> RILEY *enters; his uniform is torn; his face bleeding. He is
> dispirited and ashamed.* ERPINGHAM *rounds on him at once.*

ERPINGHAM. Another disaster to add to your ever-growing
list of failures, Riley!

> RILEY, *overcome by emotion, hangs his head.*

Your technique might have been admirable at Nuremberg,
but it's still in advance of the Home Counties. Give me
your sash and medal. You've proved yourself unworthy
of them.

> *He strips* RILEY'S *honours from him.*
> *Music: A single trumpet.*
> W. E. HARRISON *enters.*

W. E. HARRISON. They've sent a deputation, sir. They want
a word with you.

ERPINGHAM. Show them in.

> ERPINGHAM *stands to one side surrounded by his staff.*
> W. E. HARRISON *ushers in* KENNY *and* TED. TED *is fully
> dressed.* KENNY *still wears the leopard skin. He has put a
> woolly cardigan over it.*

What can I do for you, gentlemen?

TED. Mr Erpingham we won't waste time on coming to the
point. You know why we're here. The chalet area has

been locked. And, on your orders we're told, no meal will
be served tonight. Is this true?

ERPINGHAM. Perfectly true. I intend to exact reparations for
the damage done tonight.

TED. Certain elements on both sides are to blame for what has
happened. We all of us regret it. Will you be reasonable and
forget the whole sorry business?

ERPINGHAM (*with a charming smile*). I can't promise that, I'm
afraid.

TED. Why not?

ERPINGHAM. You must realise that property has been
damaged.

TED. The majority can't be held responsible for the exploits of
an irresponsible minority.

ERPINGHAM. If majorities allow themselves to be swayed by
minorities, irresponsible or not, they must take the conse-
quences.

> KENNY, *who has been listening with mounting impatience,
> explodes with rage.*

KENNY. You can't repair the damage to your property by
denying us food. Where's your logic?

> ERPINGHAM *gives* KENNY *a look of quiet contempt.*

ERPINGHAM. You stand dressed in a leopard skin and woolly
cardigan calling on logic? You're like an atheist praying
to his God.

> *The staff laugh.* KENNY *flushes angrily.*

KENNY. We want food and shelter and something to eat.
Are you going to give it to us?

ERPINGHAM. Can't you even arrive on a Peace mission
properly dressed?

KENNY. My clothes have been nicked. I can't get into my
chalet.

ERPINGHAM. Why were you using violence on a member of
my staff?

KENNY. He'd abused my wife. She's pregnant. He hit her.

ERPINGHAM. Why?

RILEY. She was screaming, sir.

ERPINGHAM. What was she screaming for?

KENNY. He asked her to. And then he hit her. I've never hit her. I agreed to waive my rights till she had the baby. I'd've killed him if I'd been left alone. It's every man's right to protect his wife.

> ERPINGHAM *smiles. There is contempt in his smile. He faces* KENNY *coolly.*

ERPINGHAM. You're talking nonsense. You have no rights. You have certain privileges which can be withdrawn. I am withdrawing them.

KENNY. You'll pay for this, you ignorant fucker!

> *There are cries of horror from the staff.*

ERPINGHAM. I think you're forgetting to whom you're speaking. Calm down before I have you thrown out.

KENNY. We want food. We demand bread. We expect shelter!

> ERPINGHAM *is made angry by the tone of* KENNY'S *voice.*

ERPINGHAM. You have damaged my property, poured scorn upon my staff and insulted me. You've cast my hospitality in my face. And yet, the bitter taste of ingratitude not dry upon my lips, you come to me with your arrogant demands. No. You must be taught a lesson. There will be no food tonight. I shall not give way. You can sleep in the open. The chalet area is closed until further notice.

TED. We'll go to the village.

KENNY. Open the gates!

ERPINGHAM. No!

TED. You can't keep us here against our will.

RILEY. Let them go, sir. Cast them into the wilderness.

ERPINGHAM. No.

W. E. HARRISON. Your stiff-necked attitude will bring untold harm. Be warned before it's too late.

MASON. Let discretion play the better part, sir.

ERPINGHAM. Never! This is my kingdom. I make the laws.

We've our traditions. And they're not to be lightly cast aside at the whim of a handful of troublemakers. I'll never agree to their demands.

KENNY. Is that the message you want us to take back to the people?

ERPINGHAM. Yes. And now get your leopard-skin legs out of here!

TED. Very well then. We'll make the best of it tonight. In the morning I intend to lodge a formal protest with the Camps and Caravans Association. Holidaymakers must be protected from people like you!

TED *and* KENNY *go off.*

RILEY. Oh, sir, (*Pleadingly.*) call them back. Let's thrash it out over a cup of instant.

PADRE. Had Pharaoh done as Chief Redcoat Riley suggests, sir, the ten plagues would not have been inflicted on the fair land of Egypt.

MASON. All avenues haven't been explored.

HARRISON. Chief Redcoat Riley has the true liberal spirit, sir. Let's give his idea a try.

ERPINGHAM (*to* RILEY). I won't have your rubbishy ideas brought into my camp. If it's your ambition to be Secretary General of the United Nations, you're at liberty to apply for the post. Personally I think you're better employed blowing up balloons for the under-fives. (*He draws himself up with dignity.*) This whole episode has been fermented by a handful of intellectuals. If we stand firm by the principles on which the camp was founded the clouds will pass. To give in now would be madness.

He takes a deep breath. He has recovered his composure.
Behave as though nothing had happened. It's my intention to defy the forces of Anarchy with all that is best in twentieth century civilisation. I shall put a record of Russ Conway on the gram and browse through a James Bond.

He turns and goes off. The STAFF *follow him.*

SCENE TEN

KENNY *and* TED *are silhouetted against the sky.* LOU *and*
EILEEN *are with them.* KENNY *addresses a crowd.*

KENNY. They have denied our children bread, insulted our
womenfolk and ignored our every plea. There is nothing
left but direct action. I say we should break open the Stores.
Take the means of supply into our own hands!

TED. No! We'd be placing ourselves outside the law.

LOU. I have complete faith in my husband. He's had a lot of
experience with disputes. He's in cakes.

KENNY. Trained locksmiths could open the food depot. It's
not difficult.

TED. We've no authority to force the locks.

KENNY. We'll take the authority then.

    KENNY *flings out his arms, embracing the crowd.*

I'm an ordinary man – I've no wish to be a leader – my only
ambition is to rest in peace by my own fireside. But, in the
life of every one of us, there comes a time when he must
choose – whether to be treated in the manner of the bad old
days. Or whether to take by force those common human
rights which should be denied no man. (*He raises his voice.*)
A place to sleep, food for our kids, and respect. That's all we
ask. Is it too much?

TED. We must behave in a reasonable manner. Our hands are
clean so far. We've acted entirely in accordance with the
law. What Ken here proposes is illegal.

KENNY. So is insulting pregnant women.

EILEEN (*weeping*). Yes. I'm pregnant. I was insulted. Made to
feel awful.

    She weeps. TED *holds up his hands and speaks to the crowd
in a calm, rational manner.*

TED. Ladies and Gentlemen. Listen to what I've got to say. Don't interrupt me. Form your own opinions and bring your intelligence to bear on the facts so that you can make an accurate decision. What are we losing? One night's sleep. One meal. I've arranged that our wives and children will have a roof over their heads. A makeshift one, it's true. Nevertheless somewhere to rest. In the morning we can make our complaints to the proper authorities. Nobody has been harmed. Let's keep it that way. We've the law on our side.

LOU *applauds. She smiles.*

LOU. My husband and I are civil defence workers. This is an emergency. We're taking over.

KENNY *addresses the crowd. His face flushed.*

KENNY. What Ted says is true. He's a good fella. We all know that. He's a reasonable man. We shouldn't forget it. But neither let us forget those pregnant women that've been insulted. And little kiddies crying for something to eat. (*Emotionally.*) Man does not live by bread alone! It's the small things in life that matter. And I'm prepared to risk a lot for those!

EILEEN *rests her head against* KENNY.

My missus and me – we've only been married a year. We're expecting our first baby. I'm terrified of anything happening to her. We're doing this thing not for ourselves, but for our wives and loved ones – pregnant now and in the times to come, that they may be safe from never knowing where the next meal is coming from. Have a bash, I say. Have a bash for the pregnant woman next door!

EILEEN *waves her hands. She jumps up and down.*

EILEEN (*screaming*). I'm in the family way!

KENNY. It's our first!

LOU *turns to the crowd.*

LOU. We're proceeding from page twenty of the Civil Defence Booklet. Will you all take up your respective positions?

EILEEN *runs across and smacks her across the face and pulls her hair. They fall screaming to the floor.*

LOU. What'y'r doing?

EILEEN. Get out of here, you silly bitch! Go on before I kick your dental plate to pieces.

TED *runs across and parts* EILEEN *and* LOU. *He lifts* LOU *up.*

TED. This is most unpleasant. (*He protects* LOU *from* EILEEN.) Stop playing the goat Eileen and behave like a grown-up.

EILEEN (*to* TED). Piss off you dirty middle-class prat! And take your poxy wife with you.

KENNY (*coming over, to* EILEEN). Did he insult you?

TED (*to* LOU). We'd better leave them to it, dear. You don't want to listen to a lot of foul language, do you?

LOU. I certainly don't. It won't make my holiday any more enjoyable.

TED *and* LOU *go off.* KENNY *and* EILEEN *stand upon the chairs.*

KENNY. To the Stores!

EILEEN. To the Stores!

Music: 'La Marseillaise'.

SCENE ELEVEN

ERPINGHAM's *office.* ERPINGHAM *is sitting reading, with a cigar in his hand and a glass of brandy beside him. There are distant sounds of cheering, breaking glass and music.* ERPINGHAM *turns a page in his book.* W. E. HARRISON *runs in.*

W. E. HARRISON. Sir! (ERPINGHAM *looks up.*) There's been a meeting in the Old Folks Wheelchair Court. A subversive element in the camp has taken the law into its own hands.

They're using deckchair loungettes to break the windows of the food store!

ERPINGHAM *puts his book down.* JESSIE MASON *hurries in.*

MASON. Oh, Mr Erpingham, they've elected a leader! There are unconfirmed reports of looting. The food store has been ransacked. And some of the younger men have started raping.

ERPINGHAM *rises. The* PADRE *enters, quickly, his face a mask of horror.*

PADRE. Oh, sir! Let us pray for guidance. Your car has been pushed into the Experienced Swimmers Only.

There is a distant noise. Rockets are heard and a sudden roar. The room is lit by a sheet of flame. RILEY *enters.*

RILEY. They've set fire to the Grand Ballroom, sir. They're marching this way.

ERPINGHAM. Who gave them permission to do these things? Switch on the public address system. I shall broadcast an appeal for calm.

RILEY switches on the address system. EILEEN's *voice is heard singing.*

EILEEN. Eee-eye, Eee-eye, Eeee-eye-O!

Under the table you must go.

If I catch you bending,

I'll have your knickers down.

Knees-up, Knees-up,

Don't get the breeze-up.

Knees-up, Mother Brown-O!!

There are loud cheers and she begins again. ERPINGHAM *switches off the address system.*

ERPINGHAM (*outraged*). Who is that woman? Sack her at once!

RILEY. She's the wife of their leader, sir. She's dancing on Mason's baby grand.

MASON gives a squeak of horror.

ERPINGHAM. Call a staff meeting. The situation must be thoroughly looked into.

RILEY. You haven't got a staff, sir. The Resident Medical Officer went an hour ago. The Chief Engineer and the Security Officer have gone within the last few minutes.

ERPINGHAM. We've lost Medicine, Science and Defence. Any more?

RILEY. The Liberal Arts, sir. Represented by the woman at the postcard stand.

ERPINGHAM. What am I left with? (*He looks at the* PADRE, HARRISON, MASON *and* RILEY.) Music, Religion and the Spirit of Independent Ireland. The cause is lost.

RILEY. Let me make a suggestion.

ERPINGHAM. No!

W. E. HARRISON. We must do something, sir. And quick.

RILEY. I was brought up, as I expect you know, in the Ancient Faith. The Faith that nurtured Raphael, gentle artist of the Renaissance. As a child I was profoundly impressed by his picture – gem of the Vatican collection – 'Pope Leo turning back the Hordes of Attilla'. You recall, sir, the calm, unwavering glance of the saint, at which the barbarian chieftain quails and gives up his avowed design of sacking the City of the Seven Hills, burial place of the Holy Martyrs?

ERPINGHAM. I know the picture well.

RILEY. Why can't we use the padre, as God used St Leo?

ERPINGHAM *considers.*

ERPINGHAM. Yes. It's not a bad idea. We'll give it a try. Have you got a crucifix, Padre?

PADRE. No, sir. I've come out without it.

ERPINGHAM. Lend him yours, Chief Redcoat Riley.

RILEY *takes off his crucifix and gives it to the* PADRE.

ERPINGHAM. Accompanied by a simple virgin – do your best, Mason – you will parley with these people. We shall await the result of your mission with interest. Off you go.

The PADRE *and* JESSIE MASON *go off.*

ERPINGHAM. My field-glasses, Riley. In the drawer.

> RILEY *takes the field-glasses from the drawer. He hands them to* ERPINGHAM. ERPINGHAM *stares through them.*

The rabble, led by their leader, approaches the very doors of Government.

> *There are faintly heard cries and the crash of falling timbers. The red glare of fire fills the room. Distant strains of 'La Marseillaise' are heard.*

With revolutionary banners flying they stream through the mists of a bloody dawn!

> *There is a sound of wood and glass being smashed.*

RILEY (*beside* ERPINGHAM). They're tearing down the Pavilion of the Judges!

W. E. HARRISON. Where will the Lady Mayoress stand for tomorrow's march past of lovelies?

> *The air is filled with smoke and flame.*

ERPINGHAM. Clothed in the glory of God the Church approaches!

> *The* PADRE, *followed by* JESSIE MASON, *cross, slowly, with great dignity. A lambent light, not of this world, accompanies them.*
>
> *Music: Gounod 'Ave Maria'.*
>
> *They go off. A sudden silence falls.* ERPINGHAM, *staring through the field-glasses, gives an exclamation of wonder.*

ERPINGHAM. Blessed are the Meek! (*He lowers the glasses and turns to* RILEY *in joy.*) A simple parish priest has quelled the anger of the politically unawakened. As the dove alighted on the Ark after the Flood, bringing hope to those within, so too he settles our fears and calms our troubled thoughts.

> *There is a sudden howl from the mob and cheers.* ERPINGHAM *looks through the field-glasses.*

Oh! Oh!

> *He turns aghast to* W. E. HARRISON *and* RILEY.

RILEY. What is it?

ERPINGHAM. The Man of God is down! Twenty Christian centuries in the dust. The Devil's Congress has belted the Lord's Annointed.

W. E. HARRISON takes up the glasses and stares. There is a squeal from MASON and cries of fright.

W. E. HARRISON. They're molesting Mason.

ERPINGHAM. She's no stranger to it. Virgin was an honorary title.

There is an explosion, and dust and plaster fall from the ceiling. They drop to their knees.

RILEY. The power plant.

The lights go out. The room is lit only by the fire outside. Smoke drifts across the room. ERPINGHAM stands and dusts himself down.

ERPINGHAM. What do you advise now, Chief Redcoat Riley?

RILEY. Flight, sir.

ERPINGHAM. I'm inclined to agree.

ERPINGHAM clears his desk of papers. He puts them into a brief-case.

W. E. HARRISON. If we can get to the Transport Section, sir, we might find the Night Porter's bicycle.

ERPINGHAM. Oh, what a dreadful experience. Remind me to ring the insurance people first thing.

The PADRE and JESSIE MASON stagger in, bruised, and bleeding, their clothes torn.

PADRE. Oh, sir, Miss Mason and I have had a dreadful experience.

ERPINGHAM. Not the same experience, I hope, Padre.

MASON. Everything is in a terrible state downstairs, sir. They've torn your Canvatex Van Gogh to shreds.

ERPINGHAM flushes with anger.

ERPINGHAM. We'll have a couple of verses of 'Love Divine, All Loves Excelling', Padre. It's fire-hoses, tear-gas and the boot from then on.

They kneel. JESSIE MASON *accompanies the hymn on her squeeze-box.*

Love Divine, all loves excelling,
Joy of Heaven to earth come down,
Fix in us Thy humble dwelling,
All Thy faithful mercies crown.

Jesu, Thou art all compassion,
Pure unbounded Love Thou art:
Visit us with Thy salvation,
Enter every trembling heart.

Come Almighty to deliver,
Let us all Thy grace receive;
Suddenly return and never,
Never more Thy temples leave.

Aaaaamen.'

They bow their heads. KENNY *and* EILEEN *and several* CAMPERS *burst into the room.*

KENNY. The time of reckoning has come.

He advances. ERPINGHAM *and his* STAFF *rise.*

What've you got to say about pregnancy now?

ERPINGHAM. Pregnancy has nothing to do with me.

EILEEN (*hysterically*). Hit him! Go on, hit him! He insulted me.

KENNY *flings aside his woolly cardigan.*

KENNY. I'm going to give you a good hiding, Erpingham. I'm going to smash your face in for the gratification of those in the family way everywhere.

ERPINGHAM. I shall confiscate your luggage. What is your chalet number?

KENNY *butts* ERPINGHAM *in the stomach.* ERPINGHAM *crumples up in agony.* JESSIE MASON *seizes* KENNY *by the arm.*

MASON. You can't do this. Mr Erpingham is a gentleman.

EILEEN *drags* MASON *away.*

EILEEN (*screaming*). We were refused permission to wed. We defied the ban on our love. I was insulted. I'm an expectant mother.

KENNY *punches* ERPINGHAM *in the mouth.* MASON *screams.* EILEEN *struggles with her. The* PADRE *tries to separate them.*

PADRE. Leave Miss Mason alone. She's a sensitive artiste.

RILEY *and* W. E. HARRISON *are fighting off the attacks of the other* CAMPERS. KENNY *is viciously beating up* ERPINGHAM. EILEEN *is screaming and hitting* JESSIE MASON. *The* PADRE *kneels amid the carnage. His hands folded in prayer.*

PADRE. Oh, Merciful Father, in Thee we trust when dangers threaten.

He is hit by an egg. The CAMPERS *and* STAFF *struggle and scream around the figures of* KENNY *and* ERPINGHAM. *Disaster strikes when* ERPINGHAM *abruptly disappears through a hole which opens up in the floor. A silence falls. They look down the hole. The* PADRE *rises and joins them. He looks down and shakes his head.*

PADRE. As the little foxes gnaw at the roots of the vine, so anarchy weakens the fibres of society.

EILEEN (*weeping*). I'm a mother-to-be. I should be protected from this kind of thing.

TED *and* LOU *enter quietly. They are awed and amazed.*

LOU. Mr Erpingham has fallen through the ceiling on to a dancing couple! There's blood all over the place.

TED. They're in pretty bad shape. Erpingham is dead.

Everybody is distressed. JESSIE MASON *weeps, dabbing her eyes with a handkerchief.* RILEY *turns to the* PADRE.

RILEY. I'll take charge downstairs, sir. Will you be able to manage up here?

The PADRE *beams.*

PADRE. Have no worries, Chief Redcoat Riley. It's Life that

defeats the Christian Church. She's always been well-equipped to deal with Death.

> RILEY *and* W. E. HARRISON *go off. The* PADRE *turns to the sorrowing* STAFF *and* CAMPERS.

As witnesses to the surprising disappearance of Mr Erpingham you will all no doubt be called upon to give evidence before the authorities. Let us remember that in the days after Christ's glorious ascension into Heaven the apostles too must've appeared before some kind of Magistrates court to account for the no-less surprising disappearance of Jesus. The gospels are silent on that memorable encounter with a Jerusalem J.P. And if, in answer to your interrogator's question, 'What happened?' you reply, 'He fell through the floor', and are rewarded with incredulity; how much nearer the hairline the eyebrows of the Magistrate to whom Simon Peter made answer, 'He went up into the air'? In small things, as in great things, the disciples were remarkable men.

> *Music: A roll of drums.*

> RILEY *and* W. E. HARRISON *enter slowly with* ERPINGHAM'S *body on a bier. They lay it across the desk.*

KENNY (*emotionally*). It was that bastard insulting Eileen. It need never have happened. (*He shakes his head.*)

TED. No matter what happens, Louie and me will back you up, Ken. You'll find the Police sympathetic. They know how it feels. Most of them have had their own wives insulted at some time or another.

LOU. If there's any question of bail Ted and me will stand as surety. We can afford the money more than you.

> EILEEN *sniffs.*

EILEEN. I'm terrified all this will affect my baby. I'd hate it to grow up warped.

> KENNY *comforts her. The assembled* STAFF *and* CAMPERS *stand round the bier. A great cross of coloured light, as from distant stained glass, falls across* ERPINGHAM'S *body. Everyone bows their heads in silence.*

Music: Bach 'Toccata and Fugue'.

RILEY. He was a great man. One of the very greatest of our time. Poet, philosopher and friend of rich and poor alike. Distinctions were foreign to his nature. He was at all times a simple man. Little children loved him.

MASON breaks down and weeps uncontrollably.

He gave up a career as a missionary to come to us. Our need is greater than theirs. It was in the Erpingham Holiday Centre that he found the spiritual peace he had long been seeking. His death, when it came, found him quite prepared. He went quietly and with great dignity.

Music fades. The PADRE speaks in a low voice at the head of the bier.

PADRE. Day by day the Voice saith, "Come,
Enter thine eternal home";
Asking not if we can spare
This dear soul it summons there.

But the Lord doth nought amiss,
And since he hath ordered this,
We have nought to do but still
Rest in silence on his will.

Music The Last Post.

Four dozen red balloons – one for each year of ERPING-HAM's life – fall slowly upon the bier. As the last balloon descends the trumpet fades. RILEY lifts his head.

RILEY. We will now file past our beloved friend and leader for the last time.

Organ music.

The mourners file past the body and go off. RILEY is left alone.

Your tie is crooked. I'll straighten it before I go. (*He straightens ERPINGHAM's tie.*) I'll have this as a relic. (*He takes the gardenia from ERPINGHAM's buttonhole.*) I'll arrange a Class A (Higher Employee) wreath, sir. I hope that will be all right?

Turns to go. Looks back.

Goodbye, sir. Be seeing you.

He goes off. The body of ERPINGHAM *is left alone in the moonlight with the red balloons and dying flames in a blaze from the distant stained glass. A great choir is heard singing 'The Holy City'.*

Curtain